THE INTELLIGENT ORGANIZATION

How to Align AI Strategy, Security, Ethics, People, and ROI for Real Business Results

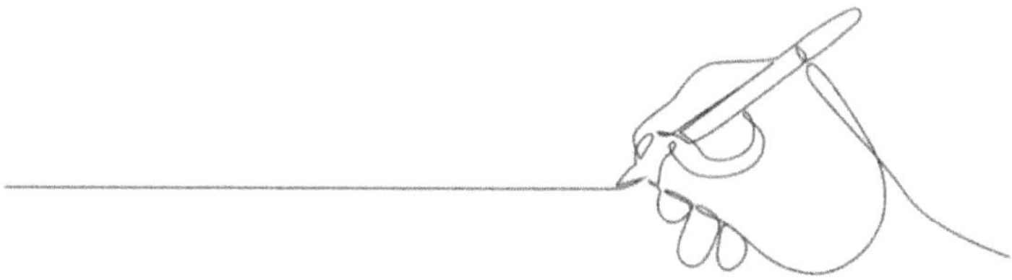

Steven Jones

COPYRIGHT PAGE

PREFACE

This book was not written to explain artificial intelligence. It was written to confront a problem.

Across industries, organizations have invested heavily in AI. They have launched pilots, tested models, and experimented with tools that promise efficiency, insight, and competitive advantage. Yet despite this activity, many of these initiatives do not move beyond early success. They stall at the proof-of-concept stage, struggle to scale, or fail to deliver the value that was expected.

This pattern is not the result of weak technology. In many cases, the systems work exactly as designed. The issue lies elsewhere. It lies in how AI is approached, how it is integrated, and how it is aligned with the broader organization.

Over time, a consistent reality becomes clear. AI success is not driven by algorithms alone. It is shaped by decisions made long before a model is deployed and long after it begins to operate. It depends on whether there is a clear strategy guiding its use, whether ethical and security considerations are built into its foundation, whether people are prepared to work alongside it, and whether its impact is measured in ways that matter.

This book is built around that reality.

It introduces a practical framework for understanding and executing AI at an organizational level. Rather than treating AI as a collection of tools, it presents it as a system that must be aligned across four critical dimensions: strategy, ethics and security, workforce readiness, and measurable value. These are not independent concerns. They are interconnected, and the strength of each determines the effectiveness of the others.

The perspective in this book is shaped by experience in AI, security, and digital transformation, where the gap between expectation and outcome is often most visible. In these environments, the consequences of misalignment are not theoretical. They appear in delayed deployments, operational inefficiencies, compliance risks, and lost opportunities. Observing these patterns over time reveals that the challenges organizations face is not unique. They are recurring, and they can be addressed with the right structure and awareness.

This is not a technical manual, and it does not require deep expertise in machine learning. It is written for leaders, decision-makers, and professionals who are responsible for turning AI from an idea into a capability that delivers real value. The focus is on clarity, application, and execution.

Throughout the chapters that follow, you will find a consistent emphasis on practicality. Concepts are explained in a way that connects directly to business outcomes. Examples are used to illustrate how challenges emerge and how they can be addressed. Frameworks are introduced to provide structure, not complexity.

The goal is not to simplify AI, but to make it usable.

Artificial intelligence will continue to evolve, but the principles that determine its success within organizations remain constant. Alignment matters more than ambition. Structure matters more than speed. And awareness, when applied early, matters more than correction applied late.

This book is an invitation to approach AI differently.

Not as a trend to be followed, but as a capability to be built with intention, responsibility, and discipline.

Because the organizations that succeed with AI are not those that adopt it first.

They are those that align it best.

Table of Contents

INTRODUCTION

Artificial intelligence is no longer a future concept. It is already shaping how organizations operate, compete, and grow. From customer interactions to security systems, from decision-making processes to operational efficiency, AI is becoming deeply embedded in the core of modern business. Yet, despite this rapid adoption, many organizations struggle to turn AI into something that consistently delivers value.

The challenge is not access to technology. It is not even a lack of data. The real challenge lies in how AI is understood, approached, and applied. Too often, organizations begin their AI journey from the wrong starting point. They focus on tools before purpose, models before meaning, and automation before alignment. This creates activity, but not direction. It produces systems, but not outcomes.

AI does not fail because it lacks capability. It fails because it lacks clarity. What separates organizations that succeed with AI from those that struggle is not the sophistication of their technology, but the strength of their approach. Successful organizations do not treat AI as an isolated initiative. They treat it as a capability that must be guided, structured, and integrated into the way the business operates. They understand that AI is not just a technical shift, but an organizational one.

At the center of this shift is a simple but often overlooked truth. AI success is not driven by algorithms alone. It is driven by how well strategy, responsibility, people, and outcomes are aligned.

Without strategy, AI lacks direction. Without ethical and secure implementation, it lacks trust. Without a workforce prepared to use it, it lacks adoption. Without measurable outcomes, it lacks justification.

These are not separate concerns. They are interconnected elements of a single system. When one is missing, the entire system weakens. When they work together, AI becomes more than a tool. It becomes a source of sustained value.

This book is built around that system.

It is designed to move beyond theory and into practical understanding. It focuses on how organizations can define clear AI strategies, implement systems responsibly, prepare their people, and measure real impact. It addresses not only how AI works, but how it should be used in a way that is effective, secure, and aligned with business goals.

The goal is not to explore every possible application of AI. It is to provide a clear path for using it effectively. A path that reduces confusion, avoids common failures, and creates a foundation for long-term success. Because in the end, AI is not defined by what it can do.

It is defined by what it is directed to achieve, how responsibly it is applied, and the value it creates over time. The organizations that understand this will not only adopt AI. They will know how to use it.

1

Why AI Strategy Starts with People, Not Algorithms

CHAPER 1: WHY AI STRATEGY STARTS WITH PEOPLE, NOT ALGORITHM

It rarely begins with clarity. More often, it begins with pressure.

Somewhere inside the organization, the conversation shifts. Artificial intelligence is no longer something to observe from a distance; it becomes something that must be acted on. Competitors are moving. Expectations are changing. The sense of urgency builds quietly at first, then all at once. What was once curiosity becomes a decision. From that moment, things tend to accelerate. Meetings are called, ideas are exchanged, and before long, a direction, however loosely defined, begins to take shape. A pilot is approved. A team is assigned. Tools are explored. There is movement, and with movement comes the reassuring feeling that progress is being made. But progress, in its early stages, can be deceptive.

Beneath the activity, there is often a lack of alignment that goes unnoticed. The initiative has energy, but not always clarity. Expectations exist, but they are rarely shared in a way that holds everyone to the same understanding. People are involved, but not necessarily prepared. And because everything appears to be advancing, very few stops to question whether what is being built has a foundation strong enough to support it.

This is how many AI efforts begin, not with failure, but with a quiet form of misalignment that is difficult to detect while momentum is high.

Time passes, and the initial confidence begins to soften. The pilot produces results, but those results are hard to interpret in practical terms. Teams interact with the system, but not with certainty. Leadership looks for impact, and what comes back feels incomplete, as though something important is missing but cannot be clearly identified.

At some point, the question changes. It is no longer about what AI can do, but why it has not done what was expected. From the outside, it may appear to be a limitation of the technology. From the inside, it feels more like a disconnect, something that was overlooked early on and has now become difficult to correct.

There is a tendency to assume that success with AI is driven primarily by capability. That if the system is advanced enough, if the investment is sufficient, if the right tools are selected, then meaningful results will follow. It is a convenient assumption because it places responsibility on something tangible, something that can be acquired, improved, or replaced.

In reality, AI does not function as a solution on its own. It behaves more like a multiplier. It takes what already exists within an organization, its clarity, its structure, its decision making, and amplifies it.

Where direction is clear, AI accelerates progress. Where it is not, AI expands confusion. Where trust is strong, AI becomes an extension of how decisions are made. Where trust is weak, it becomes something people hesitate to rely on. Where risk is understood, AI helps manage it. Where it is ignored, AI exposes it more quickly than expected.

The technology itself is rarely the source of failure. It simply makes visible what was already present.

What determines the outcome are the decisions made before the system is ever introduced. Decisions about what matters, about how success is defined, about how far the organization is willing to go and what it is not willing to compromise. These are not technical decisions. They are human ones. They reflect how the organization thinks, what it prioritizes, and how it holds itself accountable when outcomes do not match expectations.

When those decisions are made with clarity, AI has a place to operate. When they are not, even the most advanced systems struggle to become relevant. They exist within the organization, but they do not integrate into it. They function, but they do not influence the decisions that ultimately define value.

This is why any meaningful approach to AI must begin in a place that is often overlooked. Not with the algorithm, not with the tool, but with the people who will shape it, use it, and be affected by it. People determine what problems are worth solving. They decide how far a system should be allowed to go. They are responsible when outcomes fall short, and they are the ones who must trust the system enough to act on what it produces.

If that trust is not established early, it rarely develops later. If people are not prepared, they do not adapt simply because a system has been introduced. Instead, they work around it, question it, or disengage from it altogether. In those conditions, AI does not transform the organization. It becomes another layer of complexity.

Organizations that move through this differently tend to share a quieter, more deliberate approach. They resist the urge to begin with tools. They spend more time understanding what the organization actually needs before deciding how AI fits into it. They do not treat innovation, risk, and people as separate conversations. They bring them together early, even when doing so slows the initial pace.

What they build is not just an AI initiative. It is a structure that allows AI to operate with purpose. A structure that holds under pressure, that adapts as conditions change, and that provides clarity when decisions become more complex.

At the center of that structure are a few elements that consistently shape the outcome. The clarity of strategy, the strength of ethical and security foundations, the readiness of people, and the ability to translate effort into measurable results. None of these stands on their own for long. A strong strategy without trust creates resistance.

Secure systems without capable teams create friction. Well prepared people without clear outcomes create effort without direction. What matters is not the presence of these elements individually, but how well they hold together. Because in the end, the organizations that succeed with AI are not simply the ones that adopt it. They are the ones that understand how to build around it.

And that understanding does not begin with algorithms. It begins with peo

2

The Four Pillars that decide everything

CHAPTER 2: THE FOUR PILLARS THAT DECIDE EVERYTHING

There is a moment in almost every AI initiative when confidence begins to separate from reality.

At the beginning, everything feels promising. The tools are capable. The data looks usable. Early results suggest potential. There is enough progress to justify continued investment, and enough optimism to keep momentum alive. From a distance, it appears as though the organization is moving in the right direction.

But as time passes, something begins to shift. The system works, but not consistently. The outputs are useful, but not trusted.

The results exist, but they are difficult to connect to real business value. No single issue stands out clearly enough to explain the problem. Instead, it feels like a series of small disconnects, each one manageable on its own, but together creating friction that slows everything down. This is the point where many organizations begin to realize that success with AI is not determined by capability alone. Something else is shaping the outcome, something less visible, but far more decisive.

Over time, a pattern emerges across organizations that succeed and those that struggle. The difference rarely comes down to technology. It comes down to structure.

More specifically, it comes down to whether four critical elements are present, aligned, and strong enough to support the weight of what is being built.

These elements are not new, and they are not complex. But they are often treated as secondary concerns, addressed too late, or in isolation from one another. When that happens, even well-designed AI systems fail to deliver lasting impact. When they are treated as a system, the outcome changes. At its core, successful AI adoption rests on four pillars that shape how decisions are made, how systems are built, and how value is ultimately created.

The first is strategy.

STRATEGY: Without a clear sense of direction, AI becomes reactive. It follows trends instead of solving problems. Many organizations begin their AI journey with a vague objective such as improving efficiency or becoming more innovative. While these ambitions are not wrong, they are rarely specific enough to guide meaningful decisions.

A financial service firm once invested heavily in AI to improve customer experience. The initiative focused on building a recommendation engine that would personalize product offerings. The technology worked as expected. The system was able to analyze user behavior and suggest relevant services. But adoption remained low, and the impact on revenue was minimal.

The issue was not technical. It was strategic. The organization had not clearly defined what kind of customer experience it wanted to create, or how personalization would influence customer behavior in a measurable way. Without that clarity, the system operated in isolation. It produced outputs, but those outputs were not tied to decisions that mattered.

Strategy, in this sense, is not about having a vision. It is about making choices. It defines what problems are worth solving, what success looks like, and where effort should be concentrated. Without it, AI becomes directionless, regardless of how advanced the underlying technology may be.

The second pillar is ethics and security.

ETHICS AND SECURITY: This is where many organizations hesitate, often because it introduces complexity into an already demanding process. It is easier to focus on building capability than on managing risk. But the absence of ethical and security considerations does not remove risk. It simply delays its impact.

A well-known case involved a hiring algorithm developed to streamline recruitment. The system was trained on historical hiring data, which reflected years of human decision making. Over time, the model began to favor certain profiles while systematically excluding others. The bias was not intentional, but it was real. Once discovered, it raised concerns not only about fairness, but also about accountability.

The organization faced a difficult question. Who was responsible for the outcome? The system had learned from existing data. The developers had followed standard practices. Yet the result created reputational and legal risk.

This is where ethics and security intersect. Ethical design ensures that systems behave in ways that align with organizational values. Security ensures that data and processes are protected from misuse or exposure. Together, they form the foundation of trust.

Without trust, adoption becomes fragile. People begin to question the system. Decisions are second guessed. Confidence erodes, not because the system is ineffective, but because it is not fully understood or governed.

The third pillar is people

PEOPLE: This is often the most underestimated element, and the one that determines whether AI becomes integrated or remains isolated.

There is a persistent belief that AI replaces human effort. In practice, it reshapes it. Roles change. Decisions shift. New forms of collaboration emerge between people and systems. When this transition is not managed carefully, resistance begins to build.

In a global retail company, an AI driven forecasting system was introduced to optimize inventory management. The model was highly accurate, significantly improving demand predictions. Yet store managers continued to rely on their own judgment, often overriding the system's recommendations.

The issue was not the quality of the model. It was trust. The managers had not been involved in the development process. They did not understand how the system reached its conclusions. More importantly, they felt that their experience was being replaced rather than supported.

Over time, adoption improved only after the organization invested in training, communication, and transparency. Managers were shown how the system worked, where it performed well, and where human judgment remained essential. Once they understood their role within the new process, the system became a tool rather than a threat.

People do not resist technology. They resist uncertainty. When expectations are unclear and roles are not defined, even the best systems struggle to gain acceptance.

The fourth pillar is measurable results.

MEASURABLE RESULT: This is where many AI initiatives lose momentum. Early success is often demonstrated through pilot projects or proof of concept models. These provide evidence that something is possible, but they do not guarantee that it is valuable.

The transition from experimentation to production is where real challenges emerge. Systems must operate reliably, integrate with existing processes, and produce outcomes that can be measured in business terms.

A cybersecurity team implemented an AI based threat detection system designed to identify anomalies in network activity. During testing, the system performed well, detecting patterns that traditional methods missed. However, once deployed, it generated a high volume of alerts, many of which were false positives.

The result was increased workload rather than efficiency. Analysts spent more time investigating alerts without a corresponding improvement in incident response.

The solution required more than technical adjustment. The organization needed to redefine what success looked like. Instead of focusing solely on detection, it began to measure response time, accuracy of alerts, and reduction in actual incidents. The system was refined to prioritize meaningful signals over volume, aligning performance with outcomes that mattered.

Measurable results anchor AI in reality. They ensure that effort translates into value, and that progress can be evaluated objectively. Without them, initiatives drift, sustained by potential rather than impact. What makes these four pillars effective is not their individual strength, but their interaction. They form a system, one that can be visualized as a structure rather than a sequence.

Imagine a simple framework where each pillar supports the others. Strategy defines direction. Ethics and security establish boundaries. People enable execution. Measurable results confirm value. Remove any one of these, and the structure becomes unstable.

If strategy is weak, effort is misdirected.

If ethics and security are ignored, risk increases.

If people are unprepared, adoption fails.

If results are unclear, momentum fades.

The balance between these elements determines whether AI becomes a sustainable capability or a temporary experiment.

Historically, similar patterns have appeared during other technological shifts. The introduction of enterprise software in the early 2000s promised efficiency and integration. Organizations invested heavily in systems that were technically sound but often underutilized. The reason was not a lack of functionality. It was a lack of alignment between technology, processes, and people.

AI follows a similar path, but with greater impact. It does not simply automate tasks. It influences decisions. That makes the need for alignment even more critical.

Understanding these pillars is not about adding complexity. It is about recognizing where complexity already exists and addressing it deliberately.

Organizations that succeed with AI do not necessarily move faster. They move more clearly. They invest time in defining direction, establishing trust, preparing people, and measuring outcomes. As a result, their progress is more stable, and their results more consistent.

The four pillars are not a checklist to complete. They are a system to maintain. As conditions change, each element must be revisited and adjusted. Strategy evolves. Risks shift. people adapt. Metrics refine.

3

From Buzzword to Business- Defining your AI strategy

CHAPTER 3: FROM BUZZWORD TO BUSINESS – DEFINING YOUR AI STRATEGY

MOVING FROM "WE NEED AI" TO SPECIFIC STRATEGIC GOALS

There is a fundamental difference between recognizing the importance of artificial intelligence and knowing how to use it. Many organizations reach the point where they acknowledge that AI is necessary, but that realization alone does not create direction. It often leads to broad, unfocused efforts where multiple initiatives are launched without a clear connection to business value. At this stage, AI becomes a response to pressure rather than a response to purpose. Leaders see competitors adopting AI, industry conversations shifting, and expectations rising, so the organization reacts. Projects begin, tools are acquired, and teams are encouraged to "do something with AI," yet no one can clearly explain what success looks like.

This is where confusion quietly replaces clarity. Different departments interpret AI in their own way. One team focuses on automation, another on analytics, another on customer engagement. Each initiative may show promise in isolation, but together they create fragmentation. Resources are divided, priorities compete, and decision making becomes reactive rather than strategic. The organization appears innovative, but beneath the surface, it is drifting. The absence of direction does not stop activity, it simply disconnects it from meaningful outcomes.

Defining an AI strategy begins with narrowing that ambiguity. It requires translating the general statement "we need AI" into a set of specific, measurable objectives that directly affect how the business performs. This translation is not optional. It is the point where intention becomes execution. Without it, AI remains a concept that generates experimentation rather than a capability that drives results.

The act of translation forces discipline. It requires leaders to confront difficult but necessary questions. What exactly are we trying to improve? Where is the inefficiency, the risk, or the missed opportunity? How will we know if AI is making a difference? These questions shift the conversation from possibility to purpose. They remove the comfort of vague ambition and replace it with the responsibility of clear definition.

Strategic goals in AI are not abstract ambitions such as improving efficiency or enhancing customer experience. Those statements are too broad to guide action. They sound meaningful, but they lack precision. A team cannot execute “improve efficiency” because it does not specify where, how, or by how much. Strategy requires specificity because specificity enables action.

When efficiency becomes the reduction of time in a critical workflow, the problem becomes tangible. It can be measured, tested, and improved. When customer experience becomes the improvement of a specific interaction point, such as reducing response time or increasing resolution rates, it becomes something teams can design for and deliver. When security becomes the ability to detect, respond to, and prevent threats before they escalate into loss, it shifts from a general concern into a defined operational objective.

This transformation from abstract to specific is what gives AI its practical value. It connects the technology to the reality of how the business operates. It ensures that AI is not applied everywhere, but applied where it matters most.

When these goals are clearly defined, they create alignment. Alignment is not simply agreement; it is shared understanding. Teams know what they are working toward and why it matters. Decisions become easier because they are guided by a clear objective. Trade-offs can be evaluated based on their impact on the goal. Resources are allocated with intention rather than distributed based on assumptions or urgency.

Clarity also creates accountability. When goals are measurable, progress can be tracked. Success and failure are no longer subjective; they are visible. This visibility changes behavior. Teams become more focused, leadership becomes more engaged, and the organization begins to move in a coordinated way.

Without this clarity, AI initiatives tend to expand without focus, producing activity but not impact. More projects are added in the hope that one will succeed. More data is collected without a clear plan for its use. More tools are introduced without integration. Over time, complexity increases, but value does not. This is one of the most common patterns in early AI adoption. The organization mistakes motion for progress.

A focused strategy does not attempt to solve every problem at once. It recognizes that impact comes from concentration, not dispersion. By identifying where AI can create the most immediate and meaningful value, the organization creates a starting point that is both practical and strategic. This initial focus is critical because it builds momentum. Early success demonstrates value, builds confidence, and creates a foundation for scaling.

Concentration also improves learning. When effort is focused, results are clearer. The organization can understand what works, what does not, and why. This learning becomes an asset that can be applied to future initiatives. In contrast, when efforts are scattered, learning is diluted. It becomes difficult to isolate causes and replicate success.

This is how organizations move from experimentation to execution. Experimentation is necessary, but it must be guided. Without direction, experimentation becomes endless. With direction, it becomes purposeful. The transition happens when the organization stops asking "what can AI do" and starts asking "what should AI do here, for this problem, with this outcome in mind."

The strength of the strategy lies not in how much it covers, but in how clearly it defines what matters first. A strategy that tries to address everything often achieves very little because it lacks prioritization. A strategy that defines a clear starting point creates focus, alignment, and measurable progress.

In practical terms, this means resisting the urge to pursue multiple AI initiatives simultaneously without a unifying objective. It means selecting one area where the impact is both visible and valuable, and committing to it fully. It means defining success in measurable terms and aligning teams, data, and resources around that definition.

Over time, this disciplined approach compounds. One successful initiative leads to another, not through repetition, but through learning and refinement. The organization develops not just AI systems, but the capability to use AI effectively.

That is the real shift. Moving from recognizing the importance of AI to knowing how to use it is not about technology. It is about clarity, focus, and disciplined execution. When those elements are in place, AI stops being a concept that the organization talks about and becomes a capability that the organization relies on

HOW TO CHOOSE AI-DRIVEN KPIS THAT MATTER TO THE BOARD

Once strategic goals are defined, the next step is determining how success will be measured. This is where many AI initiatives begin to lose credibility, not because the systems fail, but because the measurement does. Organizations often default to what is easiest to measure rather than what is most meaningful. Technical metrics such as accuracy, speed, or system efficiency become the center of reporting, creating the impression of progress while leaving a critical question unanswered: has the business actually improved?

This gap between measurement and meaning is one of the most common failure points in AI adoption. Technical metrics describe how a system behaves, but they do not explain why it matters. A model can be highly accurate and still fail to deliver value. A system can process data quickly and still have no measurable effect on cost, revenue, or risk.

When organizations rely only on these indicators, they create what many experts now refer to as "vanity metrics," numbers that look impressive but do not reflect real impact.

While these metrics are important, they do not reflect the full value of AI. They describe how the system performs, but not what it achieves for the business. This distinction becomes critical as soon as AI moves beyond experimentation into investment. At that point, leadership is no longer asking whether the system works, but whether it is worth it.

For AI to be taken seriously at the executive level, its performance must be connected to outcomes that leadership can evaluate. These outcomes typically relate to cost, revenue, risk, and operational efficiency. They represent the core dimensions through which organizations assess performance and make strategic decisions. Research consistently shows that effective AI measurement frameworks extend beyond technical performance into financial, operational, and strategic impact, including cost savings, revenue growth, and productivity gains.

This is where a fundamental shift in thinking is required. Instead of asking how well the system works, the question becomes what has changed because the system exists. This shift may appear simple, but it fundamentally alters how AI is evaluated.

A system is no longer judged by its internal performance, but by its external effect.

Has a process become faster in a way that reduces cost or increases throughput? Has a risk been reduced in a way that protects revenue or prevents loss? Has customer behavior changed in a way that drives growth? These are the questions that move AI from a technical discussion into a business conversation.

This transition can be understood more clearly when you separate two layers of measurement. At the first layer, technical metrics ensure that the system functions correctly. At the second layer, business KPIs determine whether the system matters. Both are necessary, but they serve different purposes. Technical metrics validate capability. Business KPIs validate value.

Organizations that fail to make this distinction often struggle to scale AI. They build systems that perform well in controlled environments but cannot justify continued investment because their impact is unclear. In contrast, organizations that define KPIs at the business level create a direct line between AI activity and business outcomes. This alignment is what enables AI to move from pilot projects into production systems that are supported and sustained.

The importance of this alignment is reinforced by industry findings. Many organizations that struggle with AI adoption report a gap between perceived and actual productivity gains, often due to poor measurement frameworks and lack of outcome-based KPIs. This highlights a critical reality: without the right KPIs, organizations can believe they are improving while remaining stagnant.

A cybersecurity example illustrates this clearly. An organization deployed an AI system designed to detect anomalies in network activity. The model performed well, identifying unusual patterns with high accuracy. On paper, the system appeared successful. However, the volume of alerts increased significantly, placing additional strain on the security team. Analysts were overwhelmed, response times slowed, and overall efficiency declined.

The issue was not with the system itself, but with how success had been defined. Accuracy had been treated as the primary KPI, while operational impact had been overlooked.

When the organization redefined its KPIs, the focus shifted. Instead of measuring how many anomalies were detected, it began measuring how quickly incidents were resolved, how many threats were confirmed, and how efficiently the team could respond. These metrics reflected the real objective: improving security outcomes, not just detection capability.

This shift changed how the system was used. Alerts were prioritized based on risk, unnecessary noise was reduced, and workflows were adjusted to support faster decision making. As a result, the system began to deliver measurable value. Response times improved, workload became manageable, and the security function became more effective.

This example highlights a broader principle. AI does not create value simply by generating outputs. It creates value when those outputs improve decisions, actions, or outcomes. KPIs must therefore be designed to capture that improvement.

A second example reinforces this point from a different perspective. Consider a company implementing AI to automate customer support. The initial focus is often on efficiency, reducing handling time, increasing automation rates, or lowering operational costs. These are valid metrics, but they only capture part of the picture.

If automation reduces cost but also frustrates customers, the long-term impact may be negative. Customer satisfaction, retention, and brand perception must also be considered. This is why modern KPI frameworks emphasize a balance between financial outcomes, operational efficiency, and customer experience.

In practice, this means that effective AI KPIs operate across multiple dimensions. They measure not only what is gained, but also what is affected. Cost reduction must be considered alongside service quality. Speed must be considered alongside accuracy in real-world conditions. Automation must be evaluated alongside human experience.

This multidimensional approach reflects a deeper understanding of value. AI is not a single function; it is an integrated capability that influences multiple aspects of the business. Measuring it requires the same level of integration.

Ultimately, choosing the right KPIs is not about selecting metrics from a predefined list. It is about establishing a clear relationship between AI activity and business outcomes. This relationship must be explicit, measurable, and meaningful to decision makers.

When this connection is clear, AI initiatives gain credibility. Leadership can see how investments translate into results. Decisions become data-driven, not assumption-driven. Resources are allocated with confidence, and successful initiatives are scaled.

Without this connection, even the most advanced systems remain difficult to justify. They may demonstrate technical excellence, but without measurable impact, they struggle to earn trust at the executive level.

This is the level at which KPIs must operate. They must connect AI performance to business outcomes in a way that is clear, measurable, and relevant to decision makers. When they do, AI becomes more than a technical capability. It becomes a driver of performance, a contributor to strategy, and a measurable source of value within the organization.

PRACTICAL EXERCISE: DRAFTING A ONE-PAGE AI STRATEGY STATEMENT

Clarity in goals and measurement must be translated into a structure that can guide execution. Without this structure, even well-defined strategies can lose consistency as they move across teams and processes.

The one-page AI strategy statement serves this purpose. It is not a summary, but a disciplined way of capturing the essential elements of an AI initiative in a single, coherent view. By limiting the strategy to one page, the organization is forced to focus on what truly matters and eliminate ambiguity.

At the center of this statement is a clearly defined problem. This problem must be specific, measurable, and directly connected to a business outcome. It establishes the purpose of the initiative and provides a reference point for all decisions that follow.

Supporting this are the key elements that make the strategy actionable. The data required to build and sustain the system must be identified, along with its quality and limitations. The risks associated with the initiative, including security, privacy, and bias, must be acknowledged and addressed early. The metrics that will define success must be clearly stated, ensuring that progress can be evaluated in meaningful terms. Finally, ownership must be assigned, creating accountability for both execution and results.

When these components are brought together, the strategy becomes more than a concept. It becomes a working framework that guides implementation.

The value of this exercise lies in its simplicity and precision. It creates alignment across the organization, ensuring that everyone involved understands the objective, the approach, and the expected outcome. It also provides a basis for continuous evaluation, allowing the strategy to be refined as conditions change.

A strategy that can be clearly expressed in one page is a strategy that can be understood, executed, and sustained. Anything more complex often signals a lack of clarity rather than depth.

The movement from buzzword to business is defined by this progression. It begins with the translation of broad intention into specific goals. It continues with the selection of KPIs that reflect real business impact. And it is sustained through a structured approach that keeps the initiative aligned from start to finish. When these elements are in place, AI is no longer an abstract concept within the organization. It becomes a defined capability, applied with purpose and measured by results that truly ma

4

AI Strategy in Security - Protecting the Core

CHAPTER 4: AI STRATEGY IN SECURITY – PROTECTING THE CORE

HOW AI REINFORCES SECURITY: FROM DETECTION TO INTELLIGENT RESPONSE

At the center of every organization lies something it cannot afford to lose. It may be customer data, financial systems, intellectual property, or the operational backbone that keeps the business running. As organizations become more digital, this core becomes increasingly exposed, and the challenge of protecting it grows more complex.

Traditional security systems were built for a different era. They rely heavily on predefined rules, known threat signatures, and reactive processes. When a known pattern appears, an alert is triggered. When an incident occurs, a response follows. This model worked when threats were predictable and environments were relatively stable.

That is no longer the case.

Modern threats are adaptive. They evolve in real time, often blending into normal activity to avoid detection. Attackers do not follow fixed patterns. They study systems, exploit weak points, and move quietly within environments before taking action. In such conditions, rule-based systems alone are no longer sufficient.

This is where artificial intelligence begins to change the nature of security.

AI introduces the ability to move beyond static detection into dynamic understanding. Instead of relying only on known patterns, AI systems learn from data, observing behavior across systems, users, and networks. Over time, they establish a baseline of what normal activity looks like. From this baseline, they can identify deviations that may indicate a threat, even when no predefined rule exists.

This shift transforms how threats are detected.

Anomaly monitoring becomes one of the most powerful capabilities AI brings into security. Rather than waiting for a known signature, the system continuously evaluates behavior. A sudden change in login patterns, unusual data access, or unexpected system activity can be flagged as a potential risk. These signals, which might go unnoticed in traditional systems, become visible through AI.

Detection, however, is only part of the equation.

The real strength of AI in security emerges when it extends into response. Once a potential threat is identified, AI systems can support or initiate actions in real time. Access can be restricted, systems can be isolated, and further analysis can be triggered without waiting for manual intervention. This reduces the time between detection and response, which is often critical in preventing damage.

A financial institution applied this approach to fraud detection. Instead of reviewing transactions after they occurred, AI systems analyzed behavior in real time, identifying unusual patterns as they emerged. When a transaction deviated significantly from established behavior, it was flagged instantly, and in some cases, automatically blocked pending verification.

The result was not just improved detection, but faster containment. Losses were reduced, and the organization gained greater control over emerging threats.

This illustrates a key principle. AI does not replace security systems. It strengthens them by adding a layer of intelligence that enables earlier detection, deeper insight, and faster response.

THE RISKS WITHIN AI-DRIVEN SECURITY SYSTEMS

As AI becomes more embedded in security, it introduces a new category of risk. These risks are not always visible at first, but they have the potential to undermine the very systems they are meant to strengthen.

One of the most significant concerns is the expansion of surveillance capabilities.

AI systems, by design, require data. In a security context, this often includes user behavior, access patterns, communication logs, and system interactions. While this data is essential for detecting threats, it also creates the possibility of overreach. Monitoring can extend beyond what is necessary, raising concerns about privacy and ethical boundaries.

The challenge is not simply technical. It is organizational.

If employees feel that every action is being tracked and analyzed without transparency, trust begins to erode. Security systems, no matter how effective, become a source of resistance rather than protection. This tension must be managed carefully, ensuring that monitoring remains proportionate and aligned with clear policies.

Bias presents another layer of risk, particularly in systems used for fraud detection or insider threat identification.

AI models learn from historical data. If that data reflects existing biases, the system may reproduce them in its decisions. Certain behaviors may be flagged more frequently not because they are inherently risky, but because the data suggests a pattern that is not fully representative.

In a security environment, this can lead to unfair targeting, false accusations, or misallocation of attention. The consequences are not only operational, but also ethical and legal.

Insider threat systems highlight this challenge clearly. These systems analyze employee behavior to identify potential risks, such as unusual data access or deviations from normal activity. While effective in detecting genuine threats, they can also misinterpret legitimate actions as suspicious if context is not properly considered.

This creates a delicate balance.

Security must be strong enough to detect risk, but not so aggressive that it undermines fairness and trust. Achieving this balance requires more than technical adjustments. It requires governance, oversight, and continuous evaluation of how decisions are made.

Transparency plays a critical role here. Decisions generated by AI systems must be explainable at a level that allows them to be reviewed and validated. Without this, accountability becomes difficult, and trust becomes fragile.

These risks do not negate the value of AI in security, but they redefine how it must be implemented. They require organizations to think beyond capability and consider responsibility as an integral part of their strategy.

ALIGNING AI SECURITY WITH RISK AND COMPLIANCE FRAMEWORKS

Security does not operate in isolation. It exists within a broader structure of risk management, regulatory requirements, and organizational policies. Any AI initiative introduced into this environment must align with these existing frameworks to be effective and sustainable.

Alignment begins with understanding how risk is defined within the organization.

Different industries operate under different constraints. A financial institution must adhere to strict regulatory requirements regarding data protection and fraud prevention. A healthcare organization must prioritize patient privacy and confidentiality. These frameworks are not optional. They shape how security systems are designed, implemented, and evaluated.

When AI is introduced, it must fit within these structures rather than bypass them.

This requires integrating AI into existing governance processes. Risk assessments must include AI-specific considerations, such as model reliability, data quality, and potential bias. Compliance reviews must account for how data is collected, processed, and used by AI systems. Audit processes must be adapted to evaluate not only system outputs, but also the models that generate them. Without this integration, AI remains disconnected from the organization's core security strategy.

A global organization faced this challenge when deploying AI-driven monitoring tools across multiple regions. While the technology was effective, differences in regulatory requirements created inconsistencies in how the system could be used. In some regions, data collection practices had to be adjusted to comply with local privacy laws.

The solution was not to limit the use of AI, but to align it more closely with compliance frameworks. Policies were updated, data handling processes were refined, and governance structures were expanded to include AI oversight.

This alignment ensured that the system could operate effectively without creating regulatory risk. It also reinforced an important principle. AI in security must not only be effective. It must be defensible. This means that decisions made by the system can be explained, justified, and audited when necessary. It ensures that the organization can demonstrate not only that it is protected, but that it is operating within the boundaries of law and ethical responsibility.

AI strategy in security is not about adding intelligence for its own sake. It is about strengthening the organization's ability to protect what matters most, while managing the new risks that intelligence introduces.

It requires understanding how AI enhances detection, monitoring, and response. It demands careful attention to the ethical and operational risks that come with increased capability. And it depends on aligning these systems with the frameworks that govern risk and compliance.

When these elements come together, security evolves from a reactive function into a strategic capability. Not just protecting the organization from threats, but enabling it to operate with confidence in an increasingly complex digital environment. Because in the end, protecting the core is not just about defense. It is about trust, control, and the ability to act with certainty in the face of uncertainty.

5

Ethical Foundation - Defining AI You can trust

CHAPTER 5: ETHICAL FOUNDATION – DEFININF AI YOU CAN TRUST

WHY ETHICAL FOUNDATIONS MATTER IN AI

Artificial intelligence does not operate in isolation. Every system is shaped by the data it consumes, the assumptions built into it, and the decisions it is allowed to influence. As organizations begin to rely on AI for critical functions, from customer interactions to security decisions, a new layer of responsibility emerges. This responsibility is not something that can be added later, after the system has been built and deployed. It is embedded in every choice that is made from the very beginning, often in ways that are not immediately visible.

This responsibility is not technical. It is ethical.

What makes this distinction important is that technical problems can usually be detected, measured, and corrected within defined parameters. Ethical failures are different. They often emerge gradually, hidden within patterns of data or decision-making logic, and they tend to surface only when their impact becomes visible. By the time that happens, the consequences are no longer limited to system performance. They affect trust, reputation, compliance, and in some cases, people's lives.

Ethics in AI is often misunderstood as a constraint, something that slows innovation or complicates implementation. It is frequently treated as a checklist to satisfy regulators or a secondary concern to address once the system is operational. In practice, this mindset creates more risk than protection. When ethics is treated as an afterthought, it becomes reactive. Problems are identified only after harm has occurred, and the organization is forced into correction rather than prevention.

In reality, ethics serves a different purpose. It provides the structure that allows AI systems to be trusted, sustained, and scaled. Trust is not created by performance alone. A system may be accurate, efficient, and technically advanced, but if its decisions cannot be explained, justified, or defended, it will eventually be questioned. That questioning may come from customers, employees, regulators, or internal stakeholders, but once trust is weakened, adoption slows and value diminishes.

This is why ethical design is not separate from strategy. It is part of what makes a system viable in the long term. Organizations that integrate ethical thinking early tend to build systems that are more resilient, because they anticipate risks before they materialize. They understand that fairness, transparency, and accountability are not abstract ideals, but operational requirements that influence how systems behave in real-world conditions.

Without that structure, even the most advanced systems become fragile, not because they fail technically, but because they fail in ways that cannot be justified or explained. A model that produces biased outcomes, a system that uses data without proper consent, or an automated decision that cannot be traced back to a clear rationale does more than create inefficiency. It creates uncertainty. And uncertainty erodes confidence.

Once confidence is lost, the impact extends beyond the system itself. Teams begin to question the reliability of AI outputs. Leadership becomes cautious about further investment. Regulatory scrutiny increases. In some cases, organizations are forced to suspend or withdraw systems entirely, not because they do not work, but because they cannot be defended.

Designing AI that can be trusted begins with asking the right questions early. These questions are not abstract. They are practical, and they shape how systems are built from the ground up. They influence what data is used, how models are trained, what outcomes are considered acceptable, and who is accountable when decisions are made.

At the earliest stage, the organization must consider the origin and nature of its data. Data is not neutral. It reflects historical decisions, behaviors, and biases. If those patterns are not examined, they become embedded in the system. The result is not just a technical issue, but a continuation of past inequalities in an automated form.

The next consideration is how decisions are made and interpreted. AI systems often operate with a level of complexity that makes their outputs difficult to explain. Without deliberate effort to maintain transparency, this complexity can create a gap between decision and understanding. That gap becomes a risk, especially in environments where decisions affect customers, employees, or critical operations.

Accountability is another defining factor. When an AI system produces an outcome, responsibility cannot be assigned to the system itself. It remains with the organization. This means that clear ownership must be established, not only for building the system, but for monitoring its behavior and addressing its consequences. Without accountability, issues are more likely to be ignored or delayed.

These considerations do not slow innovation. They guide it. They ensure that systems are built with awareness rather than assumption, and that risks are addressed before they become failures. In this sense, ethics is not a barrier. It is a foundation.

When organizations approach AI with this mindset, they move beyond short-term gains and begin to build long-term capability. Systems are not only effective, but also reliable. Decisions are not only fast, but also defensible. And most importantly, trust is not assumed, but earned and sustained over time.

WHOSE DATA ARE YOU USING

Every AI system begins with data. It learns patterns, builds relationships, and generates outcomes based on the information it is given. This makes data not just a technical input, but a foundational element of the system's behavior. The question of whose data is being used is therefore more than a matter of ownership. It is a matter of responsibility.

In many organizations, data is collected over time from multiple sources. Customer interactions, transaction records, behavioral logs, and third-party datasets are brought together to create a comprehensive view. This aggregation increases the power of AI systems, but it also increases the complexity of how that data is managed.

The first challenge is consent.

Do the individuals whose data is being used understand how it will be applied? Was the data collected for the same purpose for which it is now being used? These questions are not always addressed during early implementation, yet they have significant implications for trust and compliance.

The second challenge is context.

Data does not exist in a vacuum. It reflects specific conditions, environments, and assumptions at the time it was collected. When that data is used outside of its original context, the meaning can shift. An action that appears unusual in one setting may be normal in another. If this distinction is not understood, the system may draw incorrect conclusions.

A retail company encountered this issue when using historical purchasing data to train a recommendation system. The data reflected past consumer behavior during a specific economic period. When conditions changed, the system continued to make recommendations based on outdated patterns, reducing its effectiveness and creating a disconnect with customers.

The lesson was clear.

Using data is not just about availability. It is about relevance, consent, and context. Organizations must understand where their data comes from, how it was collected, and whether it is appropriate for the decisions the AI system is expected to make.

HOW IS BIAS MONITORED

Bias in AI is not always intentional, but it is almost always present in some form.

Because AI systems learn from historical data, they inherit the patterns within that data. If those patterns reflect imbalances, omissions, or skewed representations, the system will reproduce them. Over time, these biases can influence decisions in ways that are difficult to detect without deliberate monitoring.

The challenge is not simply identifying bias, but understanding how it manifests.

In a fraud detection system, bias may appear as a tendency to flag certain types of transactions more frequently than others, not because they are inherently risky, but because the historical data contains disproportionate examples. In hiring systems, bias may emerge in the way candidates are evaluated, reflecting patterns that favor certain profiles over others.

These outcomes are not always visible at the surface level. The system may appear to function correctly, producing results that align with its training data. It is only when those results are examined more closely that patterns of imbalance become clear.

Monitoring bias therefore requires intention.

It involves testing the system across different scenarios, examining how decisions vary across groups, and identifying patterns that cannot be explained by objective factors alone. It also requires continuous evaluation. Bias is not a one-time issue that can be fixed and forgotten. As data evolves, new patterns can emerge, and existing ones can shift.

A financial institution experienced this when refining its credit risk model. Initial testing showed strong performance, but further analysis revealed that certain customer segments were consistently receiving lower risk scores despite similar financial profiles. The issue was traced back to historical data that reflected outdated assumptions.

By adjusting the model and introducing additional checks, the organization was able to reduce this imbalance. More importantly, it established an ongoing process for monitoring bias, ensuring that similar issues could be identified and addressed in the future.

Bias cannot be eliminated entirely, but it can be managed. The goal is not perfection, but awareness and control.

WHO IS ACCOUNTABLE WHEN AI FAILS

No system is infallible. AI systems, regardless of their sophistication, will produce errors. These errors may be minor, or they may have significant consequences depending on the context in which the system operates.

The question is not whether failure will occur, but how it will be handled when it does.

Accountability is often overlooked in the early stages of AI adoption. Systems are built, deployed, and integrated into workflows without a clear definition of who is responsible for their outcomes. When everything works as expected, this absence may go unnoticed. When something goes wrong, it becomes a critical issue.

Responsibility cannot be assigned to the system itself. AI does not operate independently. It is designed, trained, and deployed by people. Decisions about how it functions, what data it uses, and how its outputs are applied are all human decisions. Accountability must therefore remain with the organization. This requires clarity.

There must be a defined structure that determines who oversees the system, who validates its outputs, and who takes action when issues arise. Without this structure, responses to failure become inconsistent, and trust in the system begins to erode.

A healthcare provider faced this challenge when implementing an AI system to support diagnostic decisions. While the system provided valuable insights, there were instances where its recommendations conflicted with clinical judgment. Initially, there was uncertainty about how to resolve these conflicts and who had final authority.

The organization addressed this by establishing clear guidelines. The AI system was positioned as a support tool rather than a decision-maker, and final responsibility remained with medical professionals. This clarity ensured that the system could be used effectively without compromising accountability.

Defining accountability is not about limiting the use of AI. It is about ensuring that its use remains controlled and responsible.

ESTABLISHING ETHICAL GUARDRAILS EARLY

Ethical considerations are most effective when they are built into the system from the beginning, rather than added after deployment. Waiting until issues arise creates unnecessary risk and often requires more complex adjustments.

Guardrails provide a way to embed ethical thinking into the design and implementation of AI systems.

These guardrails do not need to be overly complex. In fact, their strength lies in their clarity and consistency. They establish boundaries within which the system operates, ensuring that decisions remain aligned with organizational values and external expectations.

At a practical level, this begins with transparency. Stakeholders should understand how the system works at a functional level, what data it uses, and what outcomes it is designed to produce. This does not require deep technical detail, but it does require openness.

It also involves oversight. AI systems should not operate without review. Regular evaluation ensures that performance remains aligned with expectations and that any emerging issues are identified early.

Finally, it requires a commitment to fairness. Decisions made by AI should be examined not only for accuracy, but for their broader impact. This includes considering how different groups are affected and ensuring that outcomes are not disproportionately unfavorable to any one segment.

A technology company implemented these principles when deploying an AI-based hiring tool. Before full deployment, the system was tested extensively for bias, its decision-making process was documented, and a review process was established to monitor outcomes over time. This approach did not eliminate all challenges, but it created a structure that allowed issues to be addressed quickly and transparently.

Ethical guardrails do not restrict innovation. They enable it to be sustained.

Designing AI, you can trust is not about achieving perfection. It is about creating systems that are responsible, transparent, and aligned with the values of the organization.

It begins with understanding whose data is being used and whether it is appropriate. It requires continuous monitoring of bias to ensure fairness. It demands clear accountability so that responsibility is never ambiguous. And it depends on establishing guardrails that guide the system from the outset.

When these elements are in place, AI becomes more than a powerful tool. It becomes a trusted one. And in an environment where decisions are increasingly influenced by intelligent systems, trust is not optional. It is foundational

6

Secure Implementation - Privacy, Bias, and Compliance

CHAPTER 6: SECURE IMPLEMENTATION – PRIVACY, BIAS, AND COMPLIANCE

IMPLEMENTING AI IN A WAY THAT RESPECTS DATA PRIVACY, FAIRNESS, AND REGULATIONS

The moment an AI system moves from experimentation into real use, it crosses an invisible boundary. It is no longer just a model producing outputs in a controlled environment. It becomes part of a system that affects people, decisions, and outcomes that carry weight. At that point, implementation is no longer a technical step. It becomes a question of responsibility.

At the center of this responsibility is data. Every AI system depends on data to function, but not all data can be treated the same way. Much of what fuels modern AI includes personal information, behavioral patterns, financial records, or operational logs. These are not neutral inputs. They represent real individuals and real activities, and the way they are handled defines whether the system can be trusted.

Respecting privacy begins with intentional limitation. It requires the organization to decide not only what data can be used, but what data should not be used. There is a tendency, especially in early stages, to collect as much data as possible under the assumption that more data leads to better performance. In practice, this often introduces unnecessary risk. The more data a system holds, the greater the exposure if that data is misused, misinterpreted, or compromised.

A more disciplined approach focuses on relevance. Data is collected and used only where it directly contributes to the defined objective of the system. Access is restricted, usage is clearly defined, and retention is controlled. These constraints do not weaken the system. They make it more sustainable.

Fairness operates alongside privacy, but it addresses a different dimension. While privacy is concerned with how data is handled, fairness is concerned with how decisions are made. AI systems do not simply process information. They interpret it, and in doing so, they can reproduce patterns that exist within the data. This is where bias becomes a practical issue.

A system trained on historical data may reflect imbalances that were never formally recognized. These imbalances can influence outcomes in subtle ways, affecting how individuals or groups are treated. The challenge is not that bias exists, but that it often remains hidden unless deliberately examined.

Addressing fairness requires continuous evaluation. The system must be observed not only for accuracy, but for how its decisions are distributed. When patterns emerge that cannot be explained by objective factors, they must be investigated and corrected. This is not a one-time adjustment. It is an ongoing process that evolves with the system.

Regulation adds a layer of structure that cannot be ignored. Across industries, expectations around data protection and system accountability are becoming more defined. Organizations are required to demonstrate how data is collected, how it is used, and how decisions are made. Compliance is not simply about avoiding penalties. It is about ensuring that the system can operate within the boundaries that define acceptable practice.

A healthcare case illustrates how these elements come together. A hospital network introduced an AI system to predict patient risk and allocate resources more effectively.

The model required access to sensitive patient information, including medical histories and treatment records. From a technical perspective, the challenge was manageable. From an implementation perspective, it required discipline.

The organization restructured its data processes to ensure that only necessary information was used. Identifiers were separated where possible, access was restricted to authorized personnel, and every use of data was tied to a defined purpose. At the same time, the system's outputs were monitored to ensure that recommendations did not disproportionately affect certain groups. Compliance teams were involved from the beginning, ensuring that the system aligned with regulatory expectations.

The result was not just a functional system, but one that could be trusted.

This is what secure implementation achieves. It ensures that the system operates within boundaries that protect both the organization and the individuals it affects.

BUILDING GOVERNANCE WORKFLOWS INTO MODEL DEVELOPMENT AND DEPLOYMENT

If privacy, fairness, and compliance define the boundaries of responsible AI, governance defines how those boundaries are maintained over time. Without governance, even well-designed systems begin to drift. Decisions become harder to explain, risks become harder to detect, and control begins to weaken.

Governance is not a layer that is added after the system is built. It is a structure that must exist throughout the lifecycle of the model. From the earliest stages of development, decisions must be recorded, reviewed, and understood. This creates a foundation that supports accountability.

The process begins with visibility. Every step in the development of the model must be traceable. Data sources must be clearly identified, transformations must be documented, and assumptions must be made explicit. This level of transparency allows the organization to understand not just what the system does, but how it arrived at its outcomes.

As the model moves toward deployment, governance introduces control points. These are moments where the system is evaluated beyond its technical performance. It is assessed for risk, for alignment with business objectives, and for its potential impact on users. These evaluations prevent premature deployment and ensure that the system is ready for real-world conditions.

Once deployed, governance does not end. It evolves into continuous monitoring. The system is observed over time, with attention given to how it performs under changing conditions. Data patterns shift, user behavior changes, and new risks emerge. Governance ensures that the system adapts without losing control.

A global financial institution applied this approach while deploying an AI-driven credit assessment system. Instead of treating the model as a static solution, they embedded governance into every stage. Data used for training was reviewed for quality and relevance. Model decisions were documented in a way that allowed them to be explained to regulators. After deployment, outputs were continuously monitored, and adjustments were made as new patterns emerged.

This approach did not slow the organization down. It allowed it to scale with confidence.

Governance workflows create consistency. They ensure that decisions are not left to chance and that every stage of the system can be examined when necessary. In an environment where AI decisions can be questioned at any time, this level of control is not optional. It is essential.

MODEL DOCUMENTATION, IMPACT ASSESSMENTS, AND RED TEAM TESTING IN PRACTICE

The practical expression of secure implementation becomes visible in how systems are documented, tested, and challenged before they are fully relied upon. These practices are often seen as supporting activities, but in reality, they define whether the system can withstand scrutiny.

Model documentation provides the foundation. It captures how the system was built, what data it depends on, and what assumptions guide its behavior. This documentation is not created for formality. It serves as a reference point when questions arise. When a decision must be explained, documentation provides the context needed to understand it.

Impact assessments extend this understanding into the future. Before a system is fully deployed, its potential effects are examined. This includes not only the intended outcomes, but also unintended consequences. How might the system affect different groups? Where could errors have the greatest impact? These questions allow the organization to anticipate issues rather than react to them.

Red team testing introduces a different kind of discipline. Instead of confirming that the system works, it attempts to break it. By simulating extreme conditions, unexpected inputs, and potential attacks, red teams expose weaknesses that would not appear under normal testing. This process reveals how the system behaves under pressure, providing insight into where it needs to be strengthened.

A well-documented case can be seen in a multinational e-commerce company implementing AI for fraud detection. The model demonstrated strong performance during initial testing, identifying suspicious transactions with high accuracy. However, the organization chose to go further before deployment.

They documented every aspect of the model, ensuring that its decisions could be traced. They conducted impact assessments to understand how different types of transactions would be treated, identifying areas where legitimate activity might be flagged incorrectly. They then subjected the system to red team testing, simulating attempts to bypass detection and introducing unusual transaction patterns.

This process revealed critical insights. Certain legitimate customer behaviors, particularly in cross-border transactions, were being misclassified as fraudulent. Without intervention, this would have created friction and reduced trust in the platform.

By addressing these issues before full deployment, the organization strengthened the system. When it was eventually launched, it achieved its objective of reducing fraud while maintaining a smooth customer experience.

This is the role of these practices. They do not exist to delay deployment. They exist to ensure that deployment succeeds.

Secure implementation is what separates AI systems that function from those that endure. It ensures that privacy is respected, fairness is maintained, and compliance is achieved without compromising performance. It introduces governance as a continuous process rather than a final check, and it reinforces the system through documentation, assessment, and deliberate testing.

In doing so, it transforms AI from a tool that works under ideal conditions into a system that can operate under real ones, where every decision matter and every outcome can be examined. That is what makes it secure.

7

AI in Security - Balancing protection and Privacy

CHAPTER 7: AI IN SECURITY – BALANCING PROTECTION AND PRIVACY

AI-DRIVEN SECURITY TOOLS AND THE WEIGHT OF THEIR DECISIONs

Security has always been about visibility and response. What AI changes is the depth and speed at which both occur. Systems that once relied on static rules now operate with adaptive intelligence, continuously learning from patterns across users, networks, and transactions. Tools such as Security Orchestration, Automation, and Response systems, user and entity behavior analytics, and real-time fraud detection platforms have redefined what it means to protect an organization.

A SOAR environment, for instance, does not simply collect alerts. It connects them, prioritizes them, and initiates actions that once required human intervention. A suspicious login, when viewed in isolation, may not trigger concern. But when combined with unusual data access and an abnormal location pattern, the system recognizes a sequence that suggests risk. It does not wait. It responds, isolating access or triggering investigation workflows.

UEBA systems operate with a different emphasis. They observe behavior over time, building a profile of what is considered normal for each user or entity. From that baseline, deviations become visible. A sudden change in working hours, a shift in access patterns, or unexpected data movement may indicate compromise or misuse. These systems do not look for known threats. They look for what does not belong.

Fraud detection systems extend this logic into financial and transactional environments. They evaluate behavior in real time, identifying patterns that suggest manipulation or unauthorized activity. A transaction that appears valid at the surface may be flagged because it does not align with historical behavior, location, or context.

These tools represent a significant leap in capability. They allow organizations to detect and respond to threats earlier, often before damage occurs. But this capability introduces a new set of ethical trade-offs that cannot be ignored.

The same systems that provide visibility can also create surveillance. Monitoring behavior at a granular level means observing how individuals interact with systems, when they access data, and what actions they take. Without clear boundaries, this can extend beyond security into intrusion.

There is also the question of interpretation. AI systems infer intent from patterns, but patterns do not always tell the full story. An employee working late on a critical project may appear anomalous. A customer making an urgent transaction while traveling may resemble fraudulent behavior. When systems act on these signals without sufficient context, they risk making decisions that are technically correct but practically unfair.

This is the central tension. The more powerful the system becomes, the more careful its application must be. Protection cannot come at the cost of trust.

AVOIDING DISCRIMINATION IN RISK SCORING, ACCESS CONTROL, AND BEHAVIOR MONITORING

The challenge of fairness becomes more pronounced as AI systems begin to assign risk. In security environments, risk scoring is often used to determine how individuals are treated. It influences whether access is granted or denied, whether activity is flagged for review, and how responses are prioritized.

These decisions are not neutral. They shape experiences and, in some cases, outcomes that affect livelihoods and reputations.

Discrimination in this context rarely appears as an explicit design choice. It emerges from the data and assumptions embedded within the system. Historical patterns, incomplete datasets, and contextual gaps can all contribute to outcomes that disproportionately affect certain groups.

Risk scoring provides a clear example. When a system assigns higher risk to certain behaviors based on past data, it may unintentionally associate those behaviors with specific groups or contexts. Over time, this creates a pattern where similar actions are treated differently depending on who performs them.

Access control systems can amplify this effect. Adaptive authentication mechanisms often adjust requirements based on perceived risk. A user flagged as high risk may face additional verification steps or restrictions. While this improves security, it can also create unequal experiences if the underlying risk assessment is not carefully managed.

Behavior monitoring introduces another layer. By continuously analyzing activity, these systems build detailed profiles of how individuals operate. When deviations occur, they are flagged for attention. The difficulty lies in distinguishing between genuine risk and legitimate variation. Without sufficient context, normal behavior that falls outside established patterns can be misinterpreted. Avoiding discrimination requires intentional design and continuous oversight. It begins with examining the data used to train and operate these systems. Data must be representative and relevant, reflecting the diversity of real-world scenarios. Where gaps exist, they must be acknowledged and addressed rather than ignored.

It continues with testing. Systems must be evaluated across different conditions to understand how decisions vary. Patterns that suggest imbalance must be investigated, even when overall performance appears strong.

Context must also be integrated into decision-making. AI systems should not operate in isolation. Human oversight remains critical, particularly in cases where decisions carry significant consequences. The role of the system is to inform, not to replace judgment.

A financial services organization encountered this issue while refining its fraud detection model. Initial deployment showed strong results in identifying suspicious transactions. However, customer feedback revealed that certain groups were experiencing a higher rate of transaction blocks despite similar behavior.

The organization responded by analyzing how risk scores were assigned. They discovered that certain patterns associated with international transactions were being interpreted as high risk without sufficient contextual adjustment. By refining the model and incorporating additional context, they reduced false positives and improved fairness without compromising security.

This illustrates an important principle. Fairness is not achieved by removing risk assessment. It is achieved by ensuring that risk is evaluated accurately and consistently.

COMMUNICATING AI SECURITY DECISIONS TO AUDITORS, REGULATORS, AND CUSTOMERS

Even the most carefully designed system will eventually be questioned. A transaction is blocked, access is denied, or activity is flagged. At that moment, the organization must explain not only what happened, but why it happened.

This is where communication becomes as important as implementation.

Auditors and regulators require clarity. They need to understand how decisions are made, what data is used, and how risks are managed. This is not satisfied by technical descriptions alone. It requires structured explanations that connect system behavior to established policies and regulatory requirements.

Transparency is essential. The organization must be able to demonstrate that its systems operate within defined boundaries, that decisions can be traced, and that mechanisms exist to correct errors. Documentation, governance records, and audit trails all contribute to this transparency.

Customers require a different form of communication. They are less concerned with the internal workings of the system and more concerned with the outcome. When a decision affects them, they need to know what happened and what they can do next.

Clarity becomes critical here. Explanations must be understandable, avoiding unnecessary complexity while still providing meaningful information. A blocked transaction, for example, should be accompanied by a clear reason and a defined path for resolution. This reduces frustration and reinforces trust.

There is also a reputational dimension. Organizations that cannot explain their decisions risk appearing arbitrary or unfair. Over time, this erodes confidence, even if the system itself is effective.

A multinational bank provides a useful case. After implementing AI-driven fraud detection, they experienced an increase in customer inquiries related to blocked transactions. While the system was functioning correctly, the lack of clear communication created confusion.

The bank responded by redesigning its communication approach. Notifications were updated to include clearer explanations, support channels were enhanced, and internal teams were trained to provide consistent responses. At the same time, documentation was strengthened to support regulatory review.

The result was not only improved customer satisfaction, but also stronger alignment with compliance expectations.

Communication, in this sense, is not an afterthought. It is part of the system. AI in security represents a powerful evolution in how organizations protect themselves. It enables earlier detection, faster response, and deeper insight into risk. But with this capability comes responsibility.

Balancing protection and privacy require more than technical skill. It requires an understanding of how systems affect people, how decisions are interpreted, and how trust is maintained. It demands careful attention to ethical trade-offs, deliberate efforts to prevent discrimination, and clear communication that makes decisions understandable and defensible.

When these elements are aligned, AI does more than strengthen security. It strengthens confidence. And in a landscape where both threats and expectations continue to grow, that confidence becomes one of the most valuable assets an organization can hold.

8

Upskilling the Workforce for the AI Era

CHAPTER 8: UPSKILLING THE WORKFORCE FOR THE AI ERA

WHY UPSKILLING IS NON-NEGOTIABLE: AI WORKS BEST WITH PEOPLE, NOT INSTEAD OF THEM

Every wave of technological change has carried the same quiet assumption: that machines will replace people. In practice, the pattern has always been more complex. Technology reshapes work far more often than it removes it. Artificial intelligence follows this pattern, but at a speed and scale that make the shift more visible and, for many, more unsettling.

What distinguishes AI from previous tools is not just its ability to automate tasks, but its ability to participate in decision-making. It analyzes patterns, generates insights, and in some cases recommends actions. This creates a new kind of working relationship between humans and systems, one where value is created through interaction rather than substitution.

The implication is clear. Organizations that treat AI as a replacement strategy often underperform, not because the technology is flawed, but because the human element is neglected. Systems are deployed without sufficient understanding, outputs are misinterpreted, and opportunities to improve decision-making are missed. The result is not transformation, but friction. Upskilling resolves this tension.

It ensures that employees do not simply coexist with AI systems, but actively engage with them. This engagement is what turns capability into performance. A model may generate insights, but it is the human who decides how those insights are applied. A system may flag a risk, but it is the human who determines the appropriate response. Without the ability to interpret and act on what AI produces, its value remains limited.

A global telecommunications company encountered this during the rollout of an AI-driven customer support platform. The system was designed to assist agents by suggesting responses and highlighting relevant information during interactions. Technically, it performed well. Yet early results showed minimal improvement in service quality.

The issue was not the system. It was the gap in understanding. Agents were unsure when to rely on the suggestions, when to override them, and how to interpret the reasoning behind them. As a result, many ignored the system altogether, reverting to familiar methods.

The organization responded by introducing targeted training focused on how the system worked and how it should be used in real scenarios. As agents became more comfortable, their engagement increased. They began to use the system as a support tool rather than a replacement, combining its speed with their own judgment.

The outcome shifted. Response times improved, consistency increased, and customer satisfaction rose.

This illustrates why upskilling is not optional. AI does not create value in isolation. It creates value when people understand how to use it effectively. In this sense, the workforce becomes part of the system, not separate from it.

IDENTIFYING ROLES THAT REQUIRE AI LITERACY VERSUS AI EXPERTISE

Not every role in an organization needs to understand AI at the same depth. One of the most common mistakes in upskilling efforts is treating it as a uniform requirement, where every employee is expected to reach the same level of knowledge. This approach is inefficient and often counterproductive.

Effective upskilling begins with distinction.

AI literacy and AI expertise represent two different levels of engagement. Literacy is about understanding. It enables individuals to interact with AI systems, interpret outputs, and make informed decisions. Expertise, on the other hand, is about creation and control. It involves building models, managing data pipelines, and refining system performance.

Most roles within an organization require literacy, not expertise.

Leaders fall into this category. They do not need to build models, but they must understand what AI can and cannot do. This allows them to make strategic decisions, evaluate opportunities, and assess risks. Without this understanding, decisions are often driven by assumptions rather than insight.

Operational roles also require literacy. Customer support agents, financial analysts, and security personnel increasingly interact with AI-driven tools. Their effectiveness depends on how well they can interpret system outputs and integrate them into their workflows. In these roles, the ability to question and validate AI recommendations becomes as important as the ability to use them.

Expertise is concentrated in more specialized roles. Data scientists, machine learning engineers, and AI architects are responsible for designing and maintaining systems. Their work defines how AI operates within the organization. They require deep technical knowledge, but they also need to understand the business context in which their systems will be used.

Between these two levels lies an important middle layer. Product managers, risk officers, and compliance specialists often act as bridges between technical and non-technical teams. They require a blend of literacy and domain knowledge, allowing them to translate business needs into system requirements and ensure that outputs align with organizational goals.

A retail organization demonstrated the value of this distinction when implementing AI for demand forecasting. Initially, training was delivered uniformly across teams, focusing heavily on technical concepts. Adoption was slow, and engagement was limited.

The organization adjusted its approach by tailoring training to roles. Executives received strategic briefings focused on decision-making. Operational teams were trained on how to interpret forecasts and adjust inventory decisions. Technical teams continued to develop deeper expertise.

The shift improved both understanding and adoption. Each group received the knowledge it needed, rather than a generalized version that fit none.

This layered approach reflects how AI operates within organizations. It is not a single function, but a distributed capability that requires different levels of engagement depending on the role.

DESIGNING AI LITERACY PROGRAMS ACROSS THE ORGANIZATION

Once roles are clearly defined, the next challenge is building a structure that supports learning at scale. AI literacy programs often fail not because of lack of content, but because of lack of design. Information is delivered without context, training is disconnected from real work, and learning does not translate into application.

Effective programs begin with relevance.

Learning must be tied directly to how AI is used within the organization. Abstract explanations of algorithms and models have limited impact if employees cannot connect them to their daily responsibilities. Instead, training should focus on practical interaction. How to interpret outputs, how to recognize limitations, and how to make decisions based on AI-generated insights.

This creates a more immediate connection between knowledge and action.

Structure is equally important. Learning should not be treated as a one-time event. AI systems evolve, and so must the understanding of those who use them. Programs should be designed as continuous processes, with opportunities for reinforcement and progression.

A simple but effective framework can be observed in organizations that approach AI literacy as a cycle rather than a checkpoint. The process begins with awareness, where employees are introduced to the role of AI within the organization and its impact on their work. This is followed by application, where learning is integrated into real tasks through guided use of AI tools. Finally, it moves into reflection, where outcomes are reviewed and understanding is refined.

This cycle creates a feedback loop that strengthens learning over time.

A financial services firm applied this approach when introducing AI-driven analytics into its operations. Rather than relying on traditional training sessions, they embedded learning into workflows. Analysts were given access to tools along with guided scenarios that demonstrated how outputs should be interpreted. Regular reviews allowed teams to discuss results, share insights, and address uncertainties.

Over time, this approach-built confidence. Employees moved from passive users to active participants, engaging with the system and contributing to its effectiveness.

Simplicity plays a critical role in this process. Frameworks do not need to be complex to be effective. What matters is consistency and clarity. Employees should know what they are expected to learn, how it applies to their role, and how their understanding will evolve.

Upskilling, when approached in this way, becomes more than training. It becomes a capability that grows with the organization.

The transition into the AI era is not defined by technology alone. It is defined by how well people adapt to it. Systems may provide speed, scale, and insight, but it is the workforce that determines how those capabilities are used.

Upskilling ensures that this relationship is productive rather than uncertain. It bridges the gap between potential and performance, turning AI from a tool that exists within the organization into one that actively shapes how it operates.

It reinforces a simple but critical truth.

AI does not replace people. It changes what they are capable of doing. And organizations that recognize this do not just adopt AI.

9

Changing Culture - Helping employees work alongside AI

CHAPTER 9: CHANGING CULTURE – HELPING EMPLOYEES WORK ALONGSIDE AI

REDUCING RESISTANCE AND FEAR WHEN AI ENTERS THE WORKPLACE

Technology rarely fails because it does not work. It fails because people do not accept it.

When AI enters an organization, it does not arrive as a neutral tool. It arrives with assumptions attached to it. For some, it represents efficiency and progress. For others, it signals uncertainty, loss of control, or even displacement. These reactions are not irrational. They are shaped by how change has historically been experienced, often with little clarity and limited involvement.

Resistance, in this context, is not opposition to technology. It is a response to ambiguity.

Employees are asked to adopt systems they do not fully understand, to trust outputs they did not generate, and to adjust workflows that once defined their expertise. Without context, this shift can feel like a loss rather than an opportunity. The instinctive response is to hold on to familiar methods, even when new tools promise improvement.

Reducing this resistance begins with clarity.

People need to understand what AI is doing within their environment and, more importantly, what it is not doing. When AI is positioned as a replacement, fear intensifies. When it is positioned as an augmentation, the conversation changes. The emphasis shifts from what is being removed to what is being enhanced.

This distinction must be communicated consistently, not just in formal announcements but in everyday interactions. Employees need to see how AI supports their work in practical terms. This is where early experience becomes critical. If the first interaction with AI creates confusion or frustration, resistance deepens. If it creates clarity or saves time, acceptance begins.

A logistics company faced this challenge when introducing AI-driven scheduling tools. Initial communication focused on efficiency gains, but employees interpreted this as a signal that roles would be reduced. Adoption slowed, and skepticism increased.

The organization responded by reframing its approach. Instead of emphasizing cost reduction, it demonstrated how the system could reduce repetitive planning tasks and allow employees to focus on problem-solving and coordination. Training sessions were redesigned to include real scenarios, showing how the tool supported decision-making rather than replacing it.

As employees experienced these benefits directly, resistance began to decrease. The system became part of the workflow, not a threat to it.

This illustrates a fundamental principle. Acceptance is built through experience, not instruction. People trust what they can see and use, not what they are told in abstract terms.

HOW AI IS USED IN PRACTICE: CUSTOMER SUPPORT, SECURITY, AND MANAGEMENT

Cultural change becomes real when it is visible in daily work. AI adoption is not defined by strategy documents, but by how individuals interact with systems in specific roles. The transition from resistance to acceptance often occurs through these interactions, where the value of AI becomes tangible.

In customer support, AI assistants have transformed how agents handle interactions. Instead of searching through multiple systems for information, agents are presented with suggested responses, relevant data, and contextual insights in real time. The role of the agent shifts from information retrieval to decision-making and communication.

At first, this shift can feel disruptive. Experienced agents may question the reliability of automated suggestions or feel that their expertise is being challenged. Over time, however, a different pattern emerges. Agents begin to use the system as a support mechanism, validating its suggestions and refining their responses. The combination of speed and human judgment improves both efficiency and quality.

A telecommunications provider observed this transition during the rollout of its AI support platform. Early adoption was uneven, with some agents ignoring the system entirely. As training focused more on practical use and less on technical explanation, engagement increased. Agents who initially resisted the system began to rely on it for routine queries, allowing them to focus more attention on complex cases.

In security operations, the interaction is more analytical. AI systems generate alerts, identify anomalies, and prioritize risks. Security analysts, rather than manually scanning large volumes of data, focus on interpreting signals and determining appropriate responses.

The challenge here is trust. Analysts must be confident that the system is identifying meaningful patterns without overwhelming them with noise. When implemented well, AI reduces cognitive load, allowing analysts to act more quickly and effectively. When implemented poorly, it creates additional work, forcing analysts to verify outputs that are not reliable.

A financial institution experienced both outcomes during different stages of implementation. Initial deployment led to an increase in alerts, many of which were not actionable. Analysts became frustrated, and trust in the system declined. After refining how alerts were prioritized and improving the quality of detection, the system became more useful. Analysts began to see it as an extension of their capabilities rather than a source of distraction.

Management roles present a different interaction. Leaders use AI not to execute tasks, but to inform decisions. Predictive analytics, performance insights, and scenario modeling provide a deeper understanding of operations. The role of the manager evolves from relying on intuition alone to combining judgment with data-driven insight.

This transition requires adjustment. Managers must learn to question outputs, understand limitations, and integrate insights into decision-making processes. When this balance is achieved, decision quality improves. When it is not, there is a risk of over-reliance or complete dismissal.

Across these examples, a pattern becomes clear. AI does not remove the need for human involvement. It changes the nature of that involvement. The effectiveness of the system depends on how well individuals adapt to this change.

LEADERSHIP BEHAVIORS THAT BUILD TRUST, TRANSPARENCY, AND PSYCHOLOGICAL SAFETY

Cultural change does not happen automatically. It is shaped by leadership, not only through formal direction but through everyday behavior. When AI is introduced into an organization, employees look to leaders for signals. How leaders speak about AI, how they use it, and how they respond to challenges all influence how it is perceived.

Trust begins with transparency.

Leaders must be open about why AI is being introduced and what it is expected to achieve. Vague or overly optimistic messaging creates skepticism. Clear communication, grounded in reality, creates credibility. Employees do not expect certainty, but they do expect honesty.

Transparency also extends to limitations. AI systems are not perfect, and presenting them as such undermines trust.

When leaders acknowledge where systems may fall short and how those limitations will be managed, they create space for constructive engagement.

Psychological safety plays an equally important role.

Employees must feel that they can question, challenge, and learn without fear of negative consequences. When new systems are introduced, mistakes are inevitable. If those mistakes are met with blame, adoption slows. If they are treated as part of the learning process, confidence grows.

A technology company demonstrated this during the rollout of AI-driven analytics tools. Instead of expecting immediate proficiency, leaders encouraged experimentation. Teams were given the freedom to explore the system, share findings, and discuss challenges openly. This approach reduced pressure and increased engagement.

Behavior reinforces message.

When leaders actively use AI tools, reference insights in decision-making, and demonstrate curiosity, they signal that the system is not optional. At the same time, when they remain open to feedback and willing to adjust, they show that the system is not beyond question.

Consistency is critical.

If leaders promote AI adoption but continue to rely solely on traditional methods, the message becomes unclear. Employees follow behavior more than instruction.

Alignment between what is said and what is done determines credibility.

Over time, these behaviors shape culture.

Trust is built when systems are transparent, when decisions are explainable, and when employees feel included in the process. Resistance decreases when individuals understand their role within the new environment and feel supported in adapting to it. Changing culture is not about forcing acceptance. It is about creating conditions where acceptance becomes natural.

It requires reducing fear through clarity, demonstrating value through real use, and reinforcing trust through consistent leadership behavior. When these elements come together, AI is no longer seen as an external force acting on the organization.

It becomes part of how the organization thinks, works, and evolves. And in that shift, the true value of AI begins to emerge. not just in what it can do, but in what people are able to do with it.

10

Driving Measurable ROI - From PoC to Production

CHAPTER 10: MEASURABLE ROI – FROM PoC TO PRODUCTION

WHY SO MANY AI PROJECTS STALL AT THE LAST MILE

The early stages of AI adoption are often marked by optimism. Teams build prototypes, test models, and demonstrate promising results in controlled environments. These proofs of concept generate excitement because they show what is possible. Yet for many organizations, this is where progress slows. The transition from proof of concept to production becomes a barrier rather than a continuation.

This stage is often described as the "last mile," but the phrase understates its complexity. It is not a short distance to be covered. It is a shift in context.

A proof of concept operates under ideal conditions. Data is curated, assumptions are controlled, and the scope is limited. The objective is to demonstrate capability. Production environments, by contrast, are defined by variability. Data changes, user behavior evolves, and systems must integrate with existing processes. The objective is no longer to demonstrate potential, but to deliver consistent value.

This difference exposes gaps that are not visible during early experimentation.

One of the most common gaps is the absence of a clear business anchor. Projects begin with the idea that AI should be used, rather than a defined outcome that needs to be achieved. As a result, the proof of concept succeeds on technical terms but lacks a direct path to operational value. When the time comes to scale, stakeholders struggle to justify the investment.

Another gap appears in integration. AI systems rarely operate in isolation. They depend on data pipelines, interfaces, and workflows that connect them to the rest of the organization. In a proof of concept, these connections are often simplified or simulated. In production, they must function reliably. Without this infrastructure, the system cannot move beyond experimentation.

There is also the question of ownership. During early stages, projects are often driven by specialized teams. When moving to production, responsibility must expand. Operational teams, business units, and leadership must all be aligned. Without this alignment, the system remains confined to the environment in which it was created.

A global insurance company encountered this pattern while developing an AI model to automate claims assessment. The proof of concept showed strong accuracy and efficiency gains. However, when moving toward deployment, challenges emerged. The model needed to integrate with existing claims systems, align with regulatory requirements, and fit within established workflows.

Progress slowed, not because the model failed, but because the surrounding system was not ready.

The organization addressed this by shifting focus from the model to the process. Integration pathways were defined, responsibilities were clarified, and operational requirements were incorporated into the design. Once these elements were aligned, the system moved into production and began delivering measurable impact.

This illustrates a critical point. The last mile is not about improving the model. It is about preparing the organization.

DEFINING REAL ROI: MOVING BEYOND TECHNICAL SUCCESS

For AI to scale within an organization, it must demonstrate value in terms that the business understands and respects. Technical performance alone is not enough. Metrics such as accuracy, precision, and recall are essential for evaluating how a model behaves, but they do not, on their own, justify investment or drive adoption. They describe performance in isolation, not impact in context. What ultimately matters is not how well the model works, but what changes because it works.

This distinction marks the transition from experimentation to real adoption. Many organizations reach a stage where their AI systems perform well in controlled environments. The models are trained, validated, and capable of producing reliable outputs. Yet despite this, the systems fail to move beyond pilot phases. The reason is rarely technical failure. It is the absence of clearly defined, measurable value.

To address this, organizations must shift their perspective. Instead of focusing primarily on model performance, they must ask a more consequential question. What is different as a result of this system being used? The answer to that question must be observable, quantifiable, and directly aligned with organizational goals. Without this alignment, AI remains an interesting capability rather than a strategic asset.

Time is often the most immediate and visible indicator of value. AI systems have the ability to reduce the effort required to perform tasks that were previously manual, repetitive, or time-consuming. This reduction manifests in shorter response times, faster decision-making, and fewer delays in processing. At first glance, this appears to be a simple efficiency gain, but its implications are broader.

Time saved is not just about doing the same work faster. It is about creating capacity. When employees spend less time on routine tasks, they can redirect their efforts toward activities that generate higher value. A customer service team that uses AI to handle basic inquiries can focus more on complex issues that require human judgment. A security team that automates alert triage can dedicate more attention to investigating real threats. In this way, time becomes a multiplier, expanding what the organization is capable of achieving without necessarily increasing resources.

Incident reduction introduces another dimension of value, particularly in environments where risk is a constant concern. In security and operational contexts, the ability to identify and respond to issues earlier can significantly reduce their impact. AI systems excel in detecting patterns and anomalies that may not be immediately visible to human observers. By doing so, they enable organizations to act before minor issues escalate into major incidents.

The value here is not only in prevention but in stability. Fewer incidents mean fewer disruptions, less downtime, and lower recovery costs. Over time, this contributes to a more resilient operation. Systems run more smoothly, teams operate with greater confidence, and the organization is better equipped to handle unexpected challenges. This form of value is often less visible than cost savings, but it is no less important.

Cost reduction is frequently the most tangible and easily communicated benefit of AI. Automation reduces the need for manual intervention, streamlines workflows, and minimizes errors that lead to rework. These improvements translate directly into lower operational costs, making them attractive from a financial perspective.

However, focusing solely on cost reduction can narrow the perceived value of AI. While savings are important, they represent only one part of a larger picture. Organizations that view AI primarily as a cost-cutting tool may overlook opportunities to create new value. They may optimize existing processes without rethinking how those processes could evolve.

This is where revenue growth becomes a critical consideration. AI has the potential to influence how organizations engage with customers, develop products, and deliver services. By analyzing data at scale, AI systems can uncover insights that lead to better targeting, more personalized experiences, and the introduction of new offerings.

These effects are often more complex to measure than cost savings, but they are equally significant. Improved customer experiences can lead to higher retention rates. More effective targeting can increase conversion rates. New services can open additional revenue streams. Over time, these contributions define the strategic value of AI, extending its impact beyond operational efficiency.

A retail organization provides a clear example of how these different dimensions of value can emerge over time. The company initially implemented an AI-driven demand forecasting system to improve inventory management. The immediate objective was to reduce excess stock and minimize the costs associated with overproduction and storage.

In the early stages, the system delivered on this objective. Inventory levels became more accurate, and waste was reduced. This alone justified the investment, as the cost savings were both measurable and immediate.

However, as the system continued to operate, additional benefits began to surface. Improved forecasting meant that products were more consistently available when customers wanted them. Stockouts became less frequent, and shelves were better aligned with demand patterns. This led to a noticeable improvement in customer satisfaction.

Over time, these improvements translated into increased sales. Customers who could reliably find the products they wanted were more likely to return, and the overall shopping experience became more consistent. What began as an efficiency initiative evolved into a driver of revenue growth.

This progression illustrates an important principle. The value of AI is not always fully realized at the point of implementation. It often expands as the system becomes integrated into the organization and begins to influence multiple aspects of performance.

Understanding this requires a broader view of return on investment. ROI in the context of AI is not a single metric that can be captured in isolation. It is a combination of outcomes that together define the system's impact. Time saved, incidents reduced, costs lowered, and revenue increased are all part of this equation. Each contributes in a different way, and their combined effect provides a more complete picture of value.

Organizations that recognize this are better positioned to scale their AI initiatives. They move beyond narrow definitions of success and adopt a more comprehensive approach to evaluation. This allows them to identify opportunities that might otherwise be overlooked and to make more informed decisions about where to invest.

Ultimately, scaling AI is not about deploying more models or increasing technical complexity. It is about demonstrating value in a way that resonates with the organization. When that value is clear, measurable, and aligned with business goals, AI transitions from an experimental capability to a core component of how the organization operates.

At that point, the conversation changes. AI is no longer something that needs to be justified. It becomes something that is expected to deliver, measured by the outcomes it produces and the impact it creates over time.

A FOUR-STEP PRODUCTION READINESS APPROACH

Moving an AI system into production is often misunderstood as a natural extension of success in testing. A model performs well, stakeholders gain confidence, and the expectation is that deployment should follow. In practice, this transition is where many initiatives begin to struggle. The challenge is no longer whether the system works in isolation, but whether it can operate reliably within the complexity of a real organization.

Performance alone is not enough. A model can achieve high accuracy and still fail when exposed to real workflows, inconsistent data, and human interaction. What is required at this stage is assurance. Not theoretical confidence, but practical certainty that the system can function consistently, integrate smoothly, and deliver value under real conditions.

This assurance is not achieved through a single test or metric. It is built through a structured approach that examines readiness from multiple angles. Each angle addresses a different form of risk, and together they create the foundation for sustainable deployment.

The first of these is alignment. Every AI system must be directly connected to a business objective that defines its purpose. Without this connection, the system risks becoming a technical success without a meaningful role.

Alignment answers a simple but critical question: what decision or outcome will this system improve?

This question must be resolved before deployment, not after. When alignment is clear, success can be measured in terms that matter to the organization. It ensures that the system is not evaluated based on its internal performance alone, but on the change it creates. Without this clarity, even a well-performing system can drift, producing outputs that are difficult to interpret or act upon.

A practical example can be seen in a customer support environment. An organization may develop an AI model capable of classifying incoming requests with high accuracy. If this model is deployed without a clear objective, it may simply categorize requests without improving response time or resolution quality. However, when aligned with a defined goal, such as reducing response time by a specific margin, the system can be integrated in a way that directly influences that outcome. Classification then becomes part of a larger process that routes requests more efficiently, creating measurable value.

The second dimension is integration. An AI system does not operate in isolation. It must exist within an ecosystem of existing tools, processes, and data sources. For the system to function effectively, it must connect seamlessly to this environment.

Integration involves more than technical connectivity. It requires consistency in how data flows into and out of the system, reliability in how interfaces behave, and clarity in how dependencies are managed. If any of these elements are weak, the system may produce correct outputs that cannot be used effectively.

Consider a scenario in which an AI model is designed to detect fraudulent transactions. If the system identifies suspicious activity but is not properly integrated into the transaction processing workflow, the insight may arrive too late to prevent loss. The model works, but the system fails because it is not embedded where it needs to be.

Effective integration ensures that outputs are not only generated, but acted upon. It connects intelligence to execution, allowing the system to influence outcomes in real time.

The third dimension is validation. Testing in controlled environments provides an initial understanding of how a model behaves, but it does not fully reflect the conditions of real use. Data in production environments is often less predictable. Patterns change, inputs vary, and unexpected scenarios emerge.

Validation addresses this gap by exposing the system to conditions that resemble reality as closely as possible. This includes testing with live or near-live data, examining how the system performs under variability, and identifying how it responds when assumptions no longer hold.

The importance of this step becomes clear when systems encounter edge cases. These are situations that fall outside the patterns seen during training but occur in real-world use. A model that performs well under normal conditions may behave unpredictably when faced with such cases.

A logistics company experienced this when deploying an AI system for route optimization. During testing, the model produced efficient routes based on historical data. However, when exposed to real-time conditions such as traffic disruptions and unexpected delays, the system struggled to adapt. Additional validation was required to incorporate these variables, ensuring that the model could handle dynamic environments.

Validation, therefore, is not about confirming success. It is about discovering limitations before they become failures.

The fourth dimension is governance. Even a well-aligned, integrated, and validated system requires ongoing control to remain effective. Governance provides the structure that ensures accountability, compliance, and continuous oversight.

This includes monitoring performance over time, documenting how decisions are made, and establishing processes for addressing issues as they arise. Without governance, systems can drift from their original purpose. Data may change, conditions may evolve, and the system's outputs may gradually lose relevance.

Governance ensures that this drift is detected and corrected. It also provides transparency, allowing stakeholders to understand how decisions are generated and to trust the system's operation.

In practice, governance often becomes most visible when something goes wrong. When a decision is questioned, the organization must be able to explain how it was made. This requires clear documentation, traceability, and defined ownership. Without these elements, accountability becomes unclear, and trust begins to erode.

These four dimensions—alignment, integration, validation, and governance—are not separate steps that occur once and are completed. They form a continuous process that supports the system throughout its lifecycle. As the environment changes, each dimension must be revisited and adjusted.

A financial services firm provides a clear illustration of how this process works in practice. The organization developed an AI model to assess credit risk, with the goal of improving decision-making in lending operations. From the beginning, alignment was established by linking the model directly to loan approval processes. The system was not built as a standalone tool, but as part of a defined decision pathway.

Integration followed by connecting the model to existing data systems and approval workflows. This ensured that outputs could be used immediately within operational processes. Validation was conducted using live data, allowing the organization to observe how the model performed under real conditions and to identify edge cases that required adjustment.

Governance was then implemented to maintain control over the system. Performance was monitored continuously, decisions were documented, and processes were established to review and refine the model as needed.

The result was not a perfect system, but a reliable one. The organization was able to deploy the model with confidence, knowing that it had been prepared for real-world use and supported by a structure that could sustain it over time.

This example highlights an important reality. Moving to production does not eliminate risk. It changes the nature of risk from uncertainty about performance to uncertainty about operation. The structured approach described here does not remove that risk, but it manages it in a way that allows the system to function effectively.

Driving measurable return on investment is what ultimately transforms AI from an experiment into a capability. This requires moving beyond the initial excitement of proof of concept and addressing the practical challenges of deployment. It demands clarity in defining value, discipline in preparing systems for real-world conditions, and alignment across the organization.

When these elements come together, AI begins to deliver results that are both visible and meaningful. It moves from potential to performance, from isolated success to sustained impact.

At that point, the role of AI within the organization changes.

It is no longer something that is being tested.

It becomes something the business depends on.

And that is what justifies not only its adoption, but its expansion into the core of how the organization operates.

11

AI in Security - Turning Automation into ROI

CHAPTER 11: AI IN SECURITY – TURNING AUTOMATION INTO ROI

FROM TECHNICAL OUTCOMES TO BUSINESS VALUE

Security teams have always measured success in technical terms. Alerts detected, threats contained, vulnerabilities patched. These metrics are necessary, but they rarely resonate beyond the function itself.

Executives and boards do not manage alerts. They manage risk, cost, and continuity. For AI in security to be taken seriously at that level, its outcomes must be translated into language that connects directly to the business.

Automation is where this translation begins.

AI-driven security systems do not simply detect threats. They accelerate how those threats are understood and handled. They reduce the time between signal and response, narrow the gap between detection and containment, and minimize the effort required to manage routine activity. These changes may appear operational, but their impact extends far beyond the security function.

Consider the dimension of time.

When an incident occurs, every minute carries cost. Systems may be exposed, operations may be disrupted, and data may be at risk. AI reduces the time required to identify and respond to these incidents, often by automating the early stages of investigation and containment. What once required manual analysis across multiple systems can now be initiated within seconds.

The value of this speed is not abstract. It translates into reduced exposure. A threat contained earlier causes less damage. A disruption resolved faster affects fewer processes. In financial terms, this becomes a measurable reduction in loss.

A global manufacturing firm experienced this shift after implementing AI-driven incident response. Prior to automation, the average time to respond to a security alert extended into hours, with multiple teams involved in validation and escalation. After introducing automated triage and response workflows, initial containment actions were executed within minutes. The reduction in response time did not just improve efficiency. It reduced the scale of impact when incidents occurred.

Fewer breaches represent a second dimension of value.

While no system can eliminate risk entirely, AI enhances the ability to detect patterns that indicate potential compromise before it escalates. By identifying anomalies earlier and correlating signals across environments, these systems prevent incidents from developing into full-scale breaches.

The business impact of this prevention is significant. The cost of a breach is not limited to immediate financial loss. It includes regulatory penalties, reputational damage, operational disruption, and long-term erosion of trust. Reducing the likelihood of breaches therefore protects multiple layers of value.

A financial services organization applied AI-driven anomaly detection across its network and transaction systems. Over time, the system identified patterns that indicated early stages of compromise, allowing intervention before data was exposed. While these events were not always visible externally, their prevention avoided costs that would have been far greater than the investment in the system.

Lower false positives introduce a more subtle, but equally important, form of value.

Traditional security systems often generate large volumes of alerts, many of which do not represent real threats. Analysts spend significant time reviewing these alerts, leading to fatigue and inefficiency. AI improves precision by filtering signals and prioritizing what matters.

The immediate effect is reduced workload. Analysts spend less time on routine validation and more time on meaningful investigation. The broader effect is improved decision quality. When attention is focused on relevant signals, the likelihood of missing critical threats decreases.

A technology company observed this when refining its AI-driven alerting system. By reducing false positives, they decreased the volume of alerts by more than half. Analysts reported improved focus and faster resolution times, while the organization benefited from more effective threat management.

These outcomes—faster response, fewer breaches, lower false positives—form the operational foundation of AI in security. The challenge is not demonstrating that they exist, but translating them into terms that reflect business value.

QUANTIFYING SECURITY ROI IN PRACTICAL TERMS

To move from operational metrics to executive understanding, outcomes must be quantified. This process begins by establishing a baseline. Before AI is introduced, the organization must understand its current state. How long does it take to respond to incidents? How many alerts are generated, and how many are actionable? What is the average impact of a breach or disruption? These measurements provide a point of comparison.

Once the system is implemented, changes can be observed.

A reduction in response time can be expressed as hours saved per incident. When multiplied by the number of incidents over a given period, this becomes a measurable efficiency gain. If faster response reduces the severity of incidents, this can be translated into avoided loss, based on historical impact.

Fewer breaches can be quantified through risk reduction. While it is difficult to assign a precise value to events that do not occur, estimates can be based on industry data and internal experience. The average cost of a breach, combined with the reduction in frequency, provides a defensible measure of value.

Lower false positives can be measured through productivity. If analysts spend less time reviewing alerts, the time saved can be redirected to higher-value activities. This creates capacity without increasing headcount, which can be expressed as cost efficiency.

A structured approach often emerges in practice.

Organizations define key metrics, track changes over time, and convert those changes into financial terms. The goal is not to create perfect precision, but to establish credible estimates that reflect real impact.

A multinational bank adopted this approach when evaluating its AI-driven security platform. By comparing pre- and post-implementation metrics, they identified a significant reduction in response time and alert volume. These improvements were translated into hours saved, reduced operational cost, and estimated avoidance of breach-related losses. The resulting analysis provided a clear view of value that extended beyond technical performance.

This is where measurement becomes meaningful. It connects system behavior to outcomes that matter at the organizational level.

PRESENTING AI SECURITY ROI TO EXECUTIVES AND BOARDS

Even when value is clearly defined, it must be communicated effectively.

Executives and boards do not engage with technical detail unless it directly supports decision-making. What they require is clarity, relevance, and confidence. The presentation of AI security ROI must therefore be structured in a way that aligns with these expectations.

Clarity begins with simplicity.

The narrative should focus on outcomes rather than mechanisms. Instead of explaining how the system detects anomalies, the emphasis should be on what changes as a result. Response times are reduced, incidents are contained earlier, and risks are mitigated. These outcomes form the foundation of the discussion.

Relevance requires alignment with business priorities.

Security outcomes should be connected to broader objectives such as operational continuity, regulatory compliance, and financial performance. This ensures that AI is not seen as an isolated initiative, but as a contributor to organizational goals.

Confidence is built through evidence.

Metrics, case examples, and comparisons provide the basis for credibility. When executives can see how performance has changed and how that change translates into value, they are more likely to support continued investment.

A structured presentation often follows a simple progression. It begins with the problem, outlining the limitations of the current state. It then introduces the solution, describing how AI addresses those limitations. This is followed by measurable outcomes, demonstrating what has improved. Finally, it connects these outcomes to business impact, showing how value is created.

A telecommunications company used this approach when presenting its AI security initiative to the board. By focusing on reduced incident response time and improved threat detection, they demonstrated how the system enhanced operational resilience. These improvements were then linked to reduced risk exposure and cost efficiency, creating a clear and compelling case for continued investment.

This approach works because it aligns technical capability with strategic understanding.

AI in security achieves its full value when it moves beyond automation and becomes a driver of measurable impact. Faster responses reduce exposure, fewer breaches protect value, and lower false positives improve efficiency. Together, these outcomes create a foundation that can be quantified, communicated, and scaled.

The transformation lies not only in what the technology does, but in how its impact is understood.

When security outcomes are translated into business value, AI is no longer seen as an operational tool.

It becomes a strategic asset. And in that shift, the conversation changes from cost to investment, from function to value, and from protection to performance.

12

The AI strategy Playbook- Putting the four pillars together

CHAPTER 12: THE AI STRATEGY PLAYBOOK – PUTTING THE FOUR PILLARS TOGETHER

FROM CONCEPT TO IMPACT: A COMPLETE AI JOURNEY

Strategy becomes meaningful only when it is applied. The four pillars introduced earlier, strategy, ethical and secure implementation, workforce readiness, and measurable ROI, are not independent ideas. They are interdependent forces that shape how an AI initiative evolves from intention to impact.

To understand how they work together, it is useful to follow a single initiative from beginning to end, not as a theoretical exercise, but as a practical journey.

Consider a midsized financial services firm seeking to improve fraud detection across its digital channels. The organization has experienced an increase in suspicious transactions, leading to both financial losses and growing customer frustration due to false alerts. The initial instinct is familiar, we need AI. But what follows determines whether this becomes a meaningful transformation or another stalled project.

The journey begins with clarity of purpose.

Rather than framing the initiative around technology, the organization defines a specific objective, reduce fraudulent transactions while maintaining a seamless customer experience. This objective anchor the entire effort. It shapes decisions, aligns stakeholders, and provides a basis for measurement.

From here, the first pillar, strategy, comes into focus. The organization identifies how AI can support its goal, not in abstract terms, but through targeted outcomes. It defines success as a measurable reduction in fraud losses, a decrease in false positives, and an improvement in transaction approval speed. These outcomes become the guiding metrics for the initiative.

At this stage, the system is still an idea, but it is an idea with direction.

The second pillar, ethical and secure implementation, emerges as the design takes shape. Fraud detection systems rely on sensitive financial and behavioral data, making privacy and fairness critical considerations. The organization defines how data will be used, ensures that access is controlled, and establishes boundaries for monitoring.

Bias becomes a central concern. If the system disproportionately flags certain customer groups based on incomplete patterns, it risks creating unfair outcomes. To address this, the organization introduces testing mechanisms that evaluate how decisions are distributed across different scenarios. Adjustments are made before deployment, not after issues arise.

Security is integrated from the beginning. The system is designed to operate within existing compliance frameworks, ensuring that it can be audited and explained. Documentation is created, not as a formality, but as a foundation for accountability.

The third pillar, upskilling and workforce integration, shapes how the system is introduced. Fraud analysts, customer support teams, and operations managers are all part of the process. They are not passive recipients of the system, but active participants in its adoption.

Training focuses on practical interaction. Analysts learn how to interpret risk scores, when to trust automated decisions, and when to intervene. Customer support teams are prepared to handle inquiries related to flagged transactions, ensuring that communication remains clear and consistent. Managers learn how to integrate system outputs into decision making processes.

This alignment reduces resistance and increases engagement. The system is not perceived as an external tool, but as part of the workflow.

The fourth pillar, driving measurable ROI, comes into play as the system moves toward production. Baseline metrics are established before deployment, capturing current fraud rates, response times, and operational costs. After implementation, these metrics are tracked and compared.

The results begin to emerge. Fraud losses decrease as suspicious transactions are identified earlier. False positives are reduced, improving customer experience. Analysts handle fewer routine alerts, allowing them to focus on complex cases. These outcomes are translated into financial terms, demonstrating clear value.

The initiative, once an idea, becomes an operational capability.

What makes this journey effective is not the technology alone, but the integration of all four pillars. Each decision reinforces the others, creating a system that is not only functional, but sustainable.

THE AI STRATEGY CANVAS: A ONE PAGE FRAMEWORK FOR ACTION

To make this process repeatable, the organization introduces a structured framework. Complexity is reduced into a single, clear view that captures the essential elements of any AI initiative.

The AI Strategy Canvas brings together five dimensions: goal, data, risk, ethics, and ROI. Each dimension reflects a critical aspect of the four pillars, but in a form that can be applied quickly and consistently.

AI Strategy Canvas

Dimension	**Core Question**	**Strategic Purpose**
Goal	What are we trying to achieve?	Defines Direction and success criteria
Data	What data powers this system?	Establishes feasibility and limitations.
Risk	What could go wrong?	Identifies vulnerabilities early
Ethics	Is this fair and accountable	Ensure trust and compliance
ROI	How will value be measured?	Connect outcomes to business

This framework does not replace detailed planning. It sharpens it.

A retail product team applied a similar structure when developing an AI recommendation system. By mapping each dimension, they discovered gaps in data quality that would have limited performance. They identified potential bias in product exposure and adjusted their approach before launch. Most importantly, they defined success in terms of conversion rates and customer engagement, ensuring that the system could be evaluated in meaningful terms. The result was not just a functional system, but a focused one.

At its core, the canvas brings together five dimensions, goal, data, risk, ethics, and ROI. These elements reflect the four pillars in a form that can be applied quickly and consistently.

The goal defines the purpose of the initiative. It answers the question of what the organization is trying to achieve and why it matters. This is not a general statement, but a specific outcome that can be measured.

Data represents the foundation. It identifies what information is required, where it comes from, and how it will be used. It also highlights limitations, ensuring that decisions are made with an understanding of what the data can and cannot support.

Risk captures potential challenges. This includes technical risks, operational risks, and broader implications such as bias or misuse. By identifying these risks early, the organization can design controls that prevent them from becoming issues.

Ethics ensures that the system aligns with organizational values and external expectations. It addresses questions of fairness, accountability, and transparency, creating boundaries that guide how the system operates.

ROI connects the initiative to business value. It defines how success will be measured, linking outcomes to financial or operational impact. This ensures that the initiative remains grounded in results.

When combined, these elements create a clear picture of the initiative. They provide enough structure to guide action without creating unnecessary complexity. More importantly, they ensure that decisions are made with a balanced perspective, considering both opportunity and responsibility.

A product manager in a retail organization used a similar framework when evaluating an AI driven recommendation system. By mapping out each dimension, the team identified gaps in data quality, clarified potential risks, and defined measurable outcomes. This clarity allowed them to move forward with confidence, reducing uncertainty and improving execution.

The canvas does not replace detailed planning. It complements it by providing a starting point that aligns teams and focuses effort.

DECIDING WHEN TO BUY AI TOOLS VERSUS BUILD CUSTOM SOLUTIONS

As organizations move from strategy to execution, a practical question often arises. Should the solution be built internally or acquired from external providers.

This decision is not purely technical. It reflects priorities, capabilities, and long-term objectives.

Buying AI tools offers speed. Established solutions come with predefined capabilities, tested functionality, and support structures. For organizations looking to address common use cases such as fraud detection, customer analytics, or security monitoring, these tools provide a faster path to implementation. They reduce development effort and allow teams to focus on integration and use.

However, buying also introduces constraints. External tools are designed for broad applicability, which may limit customization. Organizations must adapt their processes to fit the tool, rather than the other way around. There is also dependence on vendors, which can affect flexibility over time.

Building custom solutions offers control. Systems can be designed to fit specific requirements, integrate deeply with existing processes, and evolve in line with organizational needs. This approach is particularly valuable when the use case is unique or provides a competitive advantage.

The tradeoff is complexity. Building requires technical expertise, time, and ongoing maintenance. It also introduces risk, as the organization takes responsibility for performance and reliability.

A logistics company faced this decision when implementing AI for route optimization. Initial exploration focused on building a custom model tailored to their operations. However, analysis revealed that existing tools could address a significant portion of their needs with minimal customization. The organization chose a hybrid approach, adopting a commercial solution while developing specific components internally to address unique requirements.

This balance allowed them to achieve both speed and differentiation.

The decision between buy and build is ultimately a question of alignment. If the capability is core to the organization's competitive advantage, building may provide greater value. If it is a supporting function, buying may offer efficiency without compromising outcomes.

What matters is not the choice itself, but the reasoning behind it.

The AI Strategy Playbook brings together everything that has been explored throughout this journey. It demonstrates how strategy, ethics, workforce readiness, and ROI converge in practice, shaping how initiatives are conceived, developed, and scaled.

It reinforces a central idea.

AI success is not the result of isolated decisions. It is the outcome of connected ones.

When these decisions are guided by clear objectives, supported by structured thinking, and aligned with organizational priorities, AI moves beyond experimentation.

It becomes a capability that defines how the organization operates, competes, and evolves.

13

Avoiding the TOP AI Adoption Trap

CHAPTER 13: AVOIDING THE TOP AI ADOPTION TRAP

WHY AI INITIATIVES FAIL EVEN WHEN THE TECHNOLOGY WORKS

By the time an organization reaches this stage of its AI journey, the challenges are no longer about access to tools or availability of data. Most organizations today can build or acquire capable systems. Yet a significant number of AI initiatives still fail to deliver meaningful value.

The reason is rarely technical.

Failure tends to emerge from patterns that repeat across industries and use cases. These patterns are subtle at first, often overlooked during early stages when progress appears strong. Over time, however, they accumulate, creating friction that prevents initiatives from scaling or sustaining impact.

Recognizing these patterns early is what allows organizations to avoid them.

The most common traps do not appear as obvious mistakes. They appear as small misalignments that grow into larger issues. Understanding them requires attention not only to what is being built, but to how decisions are made around it.

When There Is No Clear Business Goal

One of the most frequent points of failure begins at the very start of an initiative. AI is introduced with enthusiasm, but without a clearly defined objective. The conversation centers on capability rather than purpose. Teams explore what the technology can do, but not what it should achieve.

In the early stages, this may not seem problematic. Proofs of concept are developed, models produce outputs, and initial results appear promising. The absence of a clear goal becomes visible only when the initiative attempts to move beyond experimentation.

At that point, questions emerge. What problem is being solved. How will success be measured. Why should the organization invest further?

Without clear answers, momentum slows.

The early warning signals are often subtle. Discussions remain focused on features rather than outcomes. Metrics emphasize model performance rather than business impact. Stakeholders show interest during demonstrations, but commitment weakens when decisions about scaling are required.

Course correction begins with reframing the initiative.

The organization must define a specific objective that connects directly to business value. This objective should be measurable and time bound, providing a clear basis for evaluation. Once defined, it becomes the reference point for all decisions. Features that do not contribute to the objective are deprioritized, and efforts are concentrated on outcomes that matter.

A logistics firm experienced this shift when developing an AI system for route optimization. Initial efforts focused on improving prediction accuracy, but lacked a clear link to operational performance. By redefining the goal as reducing delivery time and fuel consumption, the initiative gained direction. Decisions became more focused, and the system moved more effectively toward production.

Clarity of purpose transforms activity into progress.

WHEN ETHICS AND SECURITY ARE TREATED AS AFTERTHOUGHTS

Another common trap appears when speed is mistaken for progress. Organizations push to build and deploy AI systems as quickly as possible, driven by competitive pressure or internal urgency, with the assumption that ethical and security concerns can be addressed once the system is already in motion. At first, this approach feels efficient. Prototypes are delivered faster, results appear quickly, and momentum builds. But beneath that momentum, a different reality begins to take shape.

Ethics and security are not layers that can be added after the fact. They are part of the system's structure. When they are excluded from the design phase, the system is built on incomplete assumptions. It may function, but it lacks the stability required for long-term use. What appears to be speed at the beginning often becomes friction later.

The early signs of this problem are rarely dramatic. They appear as small gaps, easy to overlook in the rush to move forward. Data sources are not fully understood or documented. Teams rely on datasets without a clear view of how they were collected or what limitations they carry. As a result, when questions arise about the origin or quality of the data, answers become uncertain.

At the same time, decision-making logic begins to lose clarity. The system produces outputs, but explaining how those outputs were generated becomes increasingly difficult. What starts as a technical achievement gradually turns into an opaque process. Stakeholders may accept this in the early stages, especially when results appear promising, but that acceptance does not last.

Questions inevitably emerge. Why was this decision made? Why was one outcome chosen over another? Is the system treating similar cases consistently? When the system cannot provide clear answers, confidence begins to erode.

Fairness and privacy concerns follow a similar pattern. They are often acknowledged in principle but not examined in detail during early development. As deployment approaches, these concerns become more concrete. Teams begin to ask whether certain groups are being affected differently, whether sensitive data is being used appropriately, and whether the system's behavior can be justified under scrutiny. When these questions do not have clear answers, progress slows, not because the system fails technically, but because it cannot be trusted operationally.

In regulated environments, these issues become impossible to ignore. Compliance requirements demand transparency, accountability, and control. Systems that lack proper documentation or clear decision pathways struggle to meet these standards. What began as a fast-moving initiative encounters delays, reviews, and in some cases, complete redesign?

The impact is not limited to regulation. In customer-facing applications, the consequences are often more immediate.

Decisions that appear inconsistent or unexplained can affect how users perceive the organization. Trust, once weakened, is difficult to rebuild. A system that was intended to improve efficiency may instead introduce uncertainty into the customer experience.

At this stage, organizations are forced into course correction. But correction at this point is no longer simple. It requires revisiting decisions that were made early, often under time pressure, and restructuring parts of the system that are already in place. This is where the true cost of prioritizing speed over structure becomes visible.

Effective correction does not come from adding isolated fixes. It comes from integration. Ethical and security considerations must be woven into the development process itself, not treated as separate tasks. This begins with clarity around data. What data is being used, where it comes from, and how it is applied must be defined from the start. Access must be controlled in a way that reflects both operational needs and privacy requirements.

Decision logic must also be made visible. Systems should not only produce results, but allow those results to be understood. This does not require simplifying complex models, but it does require creating pathways for explanation. When a decision is made, there must be a way to trace how that decision was reached.

Testing must extend beyond performance. Accuracy alone does not capture how a system behaves under real conditions. Systems must be examined for fairness, ensuring that outcomes are consistent across different scenarios. They must be tested for resilience, identifying how they respond when inputs change or when unexpected situations arise.

Governance provides the structure that holds these elements together. It establishes how systems are monitored, how decisions are documented, and how issues are addressed over time. Without governance, even well-designed systems can drift, gradually moving away from their intended purpose.

A healthcare provider offers a clear illustration of how this dynamic unfolds. The organization developed an AI system designed to prioritize patients based on risk, with the goal of improving care delivery. Early development focused heavily on predictive accuracy. The model performed well, identifying high-risk cases with strong reliability. Encouraged by these results, the organization moved toward deployment.

As the system approached real use, new questions began to surface. Clinicians asked how the system determined priority levels. Patients raised concerns about fairness and transparency. Regulators required assurance that decisions could be explained and justified. These questions revealed gaps that had not been addressed during development.

The organization made the decision to pause deployment. This was not a failure, but a recognition that the system was not yet ready for the environment it was entering. Additional work was undertaken to document data sources, clarify decision pathways, and introduce checks that ensured fairness across different patient groups. Governance processes were established to monitor the system once deployed.

This delay carried a cost in time, but it prevented a far greater cost in risk. When the system was eventually implemented, it operated with both effectiveness and accountability. Clinicians understood how to use it, patients could trust its outcomes, and regulators could evaluate its behavior with confidence.

The lesson is direct. Addressing ethics and security early does not slow progress. It defines the kind of progress that can be sustained.

When these considerations are embedded from the beginning, they shape how systems are built, how decisions are made, and how outcomes are evaluated. They reduce uncertainty, strengthen trust, and allow organizations to move forward without the need for constant correction.

Speed, when guided by structure, leads to momentum.

Speed without structure leads to rework.

And in the context of AI, where decisions carry real consequences, the difference between the two is what determines whether an initiative succeeds or struggles to move forward.

WHEN UPSKILLING IS SKIPPED OR UNDERVALUED

Technology adoption is often approached as a deployment exercise. Systems are introduced, and employees are expected to adapt. Training may be provided, but it is frequently limited in scope or treated as a secondary activity.

This creates a disconnect.

AI systems change how work is performed, but without sufficient understanding, employees struggle to integrate them into their routines. Outputs are misinterpreted, tools are underused, and confidence declines. The system may function as designed, but its value is not realized.

The early warning signals appear in behavior. Employees revert to previous methods even when new tools are available. Usage remains inconsistent across teams. Feedback reflects uncertainty rather than engagement. Over time, the system becomes marginal to operations rather than central.

Course correction requires a shift in perspective.

Upskilling must be treated as part of the system, not an addition to it. Training should be practical, role specific, and continuous. Employees need to understand not only how to use AI tools, but how those tools fit into their decision-making processes.

A financial services firm encountered this challenge when introducing AI driven analytics. Initial adoption was low, despite the system's capabilities. By redesigning training to focus on real scenarios and integrating learning into daily workflows, the organization increased engagement. Employees began to use the system actively, and its impact became visible.

Understanding drives adoption.

WHEN THERE IS NO PLAN FOR ROI BEYOND THE PILOT

The final trap appears when initiatives succeed in early stages but lack a path to sustained value. Proofs of concept demonstrate capability, but there is no clear plan for how value will be measured or maintained after deployment.

This creates a plateau.

The system exists, but its impact is unclear. Investment decisions become difficult, and support begins to weaken. Without measurable outcomes, the initiative struggles to justify its continuation.

The early warning signals include a focus on technical metrics without corresponding business measures. Reports highlight model performance, but do not connect it to operational or financial impact. Stakeholders express interest, but questions about value remain unresolved.

Course correction begins with measurement.

Organizations must define how value will be quantified before scaling. This includes establishing baseline metrics, identifying key outcomes, and linking those outcomes to business objectives. Measurement should continue after deployment, ensuring that value is tracked and communicated over time.

A retail company faced this issue after implementing an AI driven recommendation system. While the system improved personalization, its impact on revenue was not clearly defined. By introducing metrics that tracked conversion rates and customer engagement, the organization was able to demonstrate value and secure continued investment.

Value must be visible to be sustained.

TURNING AWARENESS INTO ADVANTAGE

Avoiding these traps does not require perfect execution. It requires awareness, discipline, and the ability to respond before small gaps grow into structural weaknesses. In many organizations, failure in AI initiatives does not come from a lack of ambition or investment. It comes from misalignment that is allowed to persist unnoticed. What begins as a vague goal, an overlooked ethical concern, a delayed training effort, or an undefined measure of value gradually compounds into something much harder to correct.

Each of these patterns represents a disconnect between what the organization intends to achieve and how it is actually operating. When the goal is unclear, teams move in different directions, and effort becomes fragmented. When ethics and security are not integrated early, risks accumulate silently until they surface in ways that damage trust. When people are not prepared to work with AI, adoption slows, and resistance begins to form. When value is not clearly defined, progress becomes difficult to measure, and initiatives struggle to move beyond experimentation.

What makes these gaps particularly dangerous is that they rarely appear as immediate failure. They develop gradually. Progress may still be visible, but it becomes inconsistent. Outputs are produced, but outcomes are unclear. Over time, this creates a pattern where activity increases but impact does not. To better understand this, it helps to see AI adoption not as a straight line, but as a system of reinforcing elements. When one element weakens, it affects the others.

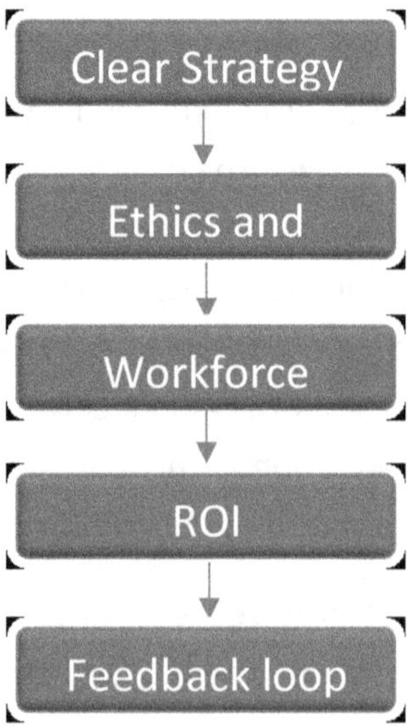

In this flow, strategy defines direction. Ethics and security protect that direction from risk. Workforce readiness ensures that the system can operate effectively. ROI validates the effort and provides the basis for scaling. The feedback loop then feeds insight back into strategy, allowing the cycle to improve over time.

If any part of this system is weak, the entire cycle is affected. A strong model without trained people will not be used effectively. A well-trained workforce without clear ROI will not sustain investment. A high-performing system without ethical grounding will eventually face resistance or regulatory pressure. The system only works when all parts move together.

This is why awareness is so powerful.

Organizations that succeed with AI do not eliminate challenges. They recognize patterns early and respond before those patterns solidify. They understand that small misalignments, if left unaddressed, eventually become barriers. But when addressed early, they become points of adjustment that strengthen the system.

Consider the difference in trajectory.

An organization that ignores early signs of misalignment often finds itself reacting late. At that point, changes are more disruptive, more expensive, and less effective. In contrast, an organization that remains attentive is able to make small, continuous corrections. These corrections are less visible, but they are far more powerful over time.

This creates two very different outcomes.

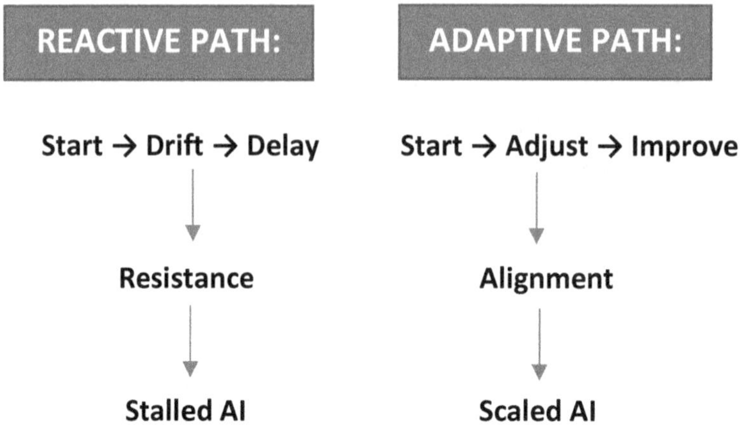

The reactive path is characterized by late recognition and larger corrections. The adaptive path is defined by early awareness and continuous alignment. The difference between the two is not capability, but attention.

AI adoption, by its nature, is iterative. It requires testing, learning, and refining. Mistakes are part of that process, but they do not have to define the outcome. When organizations treat mistakes as signals rather than failures, they gain insight into how the system is behaving. That insight becomes the basis for improvement.

This is where advantage begins to form.

Awareness, when combined with structure, creates control. It allows organizations to move with intention rather than reaction. Strategy becomes clearer because it is continuously refined. Trust is strengthened because risks are addressed before they escalate. People become more engaged because they are prepared and supported. Value becomes visible because it is measured and communicated effectively.

Over time, this alignment builds momentum.

AI initiatives no longer depend on isolated success. They become part of how the organization operates. They evolve with changing conditions, scale with confidence, and continue to deliver value beyond initial deployment. In this sense, awareness is not just a defensive capability. It is a strategic advantage. Because the organizations that pay attention early do not just avoid failure.

They position themselves to sustain success.

14

The AI Ready Leader - Your Personal AI Leadership Plan

CJAPTER 14: THE AI READY LEADER – YOUR PERSONAL AI LEADERSHIP PLAN

WHAT IT MEANS TO BE AN AI READY LEADER

The final stage of AI adoption is not defined by systems, frameworks, or even outcomes. It is defined by leadership.

Technology can be acquired. Processes can be designed. Skills can be developed. But without the right leadership mindset, these elements remain disconnected. The organization may experiment with AI, but it will struggle to sustain momentum or scale impact.

An AI ready leader does not need to be a technical expert. The role is not to build models or write algorithms. It is to create the conditions under which AI can succeed.

This begins with curiosity.

AI introduces new ways of working, new forms of insight, and new types of risk. Leaders who approach it with fixed assumptions often limit its potential. They see AI as either a solution to everything or a threat to stability. Neither perspective creates progress. Curiosity, by contrast, creates space for exploration. It allows leaders to ask better questions, challenge initial conclusions, and remain open to learning.

Curiosity is not passive interest. It is active engagement.

A leader who is curious does not simply approve AI initiatives. They seek to understand how these initiatives work, what they require, and how they affect the organization. They engage with teams, ask for clarity, and remain involved as systems evolve.

Alongside curiosity sits responsibility.

AI systems influence decisions that affect customers, employees, and operations. This influence carries ethical implications. Leaders must ensure that systems are designed and used in ways that align with organizational values. This requires attention to fairness, transparency, and accountability.

An ethical leader does not treat these considerations as constraints. They treat them as foundations.

They ask where data comes from, how decisions are made, and who is affected by those decisions. They ensure that risks are acknowledged and managed, not overlooked in pursuit of speed.

The third dimension is focus on results.

AI initiatives often begin with exploration, but they must lead to outcomes. Leaders must maintain a clear connection between activity and value. This requires discipline. It means defining what success looks like, tracking progress, and making adjustments when results do not align with expectations.

A results focused leader does not measure success by the number of systems deployed. They measure it by the impact those systems create.

When these three qualities come together, curiosity, ethical responsibility, and focus on results, leadership becomes the force that aligns strategy, execution, and impact.

A SIMPLE WEEKLY PRACTICE TO KEEP AI ON TRACK

Leadership is not defined by occasional decisions. It is defined by consistent attention.

AI initiatives evolve quickly. Data changes, systems adapt, and new challenges emerge. Without regular review, small issues can grow into larger problems. A simple, structured practice helps maintain alignment and ensures that initiatives remain on course.

This practice does not require extensive time or complex reporting. It requires focus.

Each week, the leader revisits three dimensions of the initiative.

The first is data.

The question here is not only whether the system is functioning, but whether the data it relies on remains relevant and reliable. Has anything changed in how data is generated or collected? Are there signs that quality has shifted. Are outputs still aligned with expectations.

This review keeps attention on the foundation of the system. AI is only as effective as the data it uses, and changes in data often signal changes in performance.

The second dimension is risk.

Every AI system carries risk, whether technical, operational, or ethical. A weekly review ensures that these risks are not static assumptions but actively managed elements. Are there new vulnerabilities. Have any unexpected behaviors emerged? Are existing controls still sufficient.

This is where leadership reinforces accountability. Risks are not eliminated, but they are monitored and addressed.

The third dimension is people.

AI changes how work is performed, and its success depends on how individuals engage with it. Are teams using the system effectively. Is there confusion or resistance. Are there opportunities to improve understanding or integration.

This review connects the system to the workforce. It ensures that adoption remains active, not assumed.

Over time, this practice creates a rhythm. It keeps the initiative visible, maintains alignment, and allows adjustments to be made before issues become significant. It also reinforces a culture of continuous improvement, where systems are not static but evolving.

Your Personal AI Leadership Action Plan

Understanding principles is important, but leadership becomes real through action. At this stage, the focus shifts from the organization to the individual. The question is no longer how AI initiatives should be managed in theory, but how one leader applies these ideas in practice.

The most effective way to begin is with a single initiative.

This does not need to be the largest or most complex project. It needs to be meaningful enough to demonstrate impact and manageable enough to allow focused attention. By concentrating on one initiative, the leader creates clarity and avoids dilution of effort.

The next step is to apply the four pillars.

The leader defines the objective, ensuring that it is specific and measurable. This establishes direction and provides a basis for evaluation. Without this clarity, progress becomes difficult to assess.

The leader then examines how the system will be implemented. Data sources are identified, ethical considerations are addressed, and security requirements are defined. This ensures that the system is built on a foundation that supports trust and compliance.

Attention then turns to people.

The leader considers how the initiative will affect those who interact with it. What do they need to understand? How will their roles change? What support is required to ensure that they can engage effectively.

Finally, the leader defines how value will be measured.

This includes identifying key metrics, establishing baselines, and determining how outcomes will be tracked over time. Value is not assumed. It is observed and communicated.

Once these elements are in place, the initiative moves forward with structure and clarity. Progress is reviewed regularly using the weekly practice. Adjustments are made as needed. Successes are recognized, and challenges are addressed. Over time, this approach creates more than a successful project.

It develops capability.

The leader gains experience in aligning strategy with execution, balancing opportunity with responsibility, and connecting technology to value. This experience can then be applied to other initiatives, creating a cycle of improvement that extends across the organization.

The AI ready leader is not defined by technical expertise, but by the ability to guide transformation.

They remain curious in the face of change, grounded in ethical responsibility, and focused on results that matter. They create structure without limiting innovation and maintain clarity without oversimplifying complexity.

Most importantly, they act.

Because AI does not transform organizations on its own.

Leaders do. And those who take ownership of this role do not simply adopt AI. They shape how it defines the future of their organization.

CONCLUSION: BUILDING WHAT LASTS

Artificial intelligence has moved beyond possibility. It is no longer a question of whether organizations will adopt AI, but how well they will do it. Throughout this book, one idea has remained constant: AI success is not defined by technology alone. It is defined by how clearly it is directed, how responsibly it is implemented, how well people are prepared for it, and how consistently it delivers value.

What begins as a technological initiative quickly becomes something broader. It becomes a test of leadership, discipline, and organizational alignment.

The organizations that succeed with AI are not the ones that move the fastest or adopt the most tools. They are the ones that understand what they are trying to achieve and why it matters. They do not treat AI as an isolated project, but as a capability that must be integrated into how the business operates. This distinction changes everything. It shifts AI from experimentation to execution, from activity to impact.

At the center of this transformation are the four pillars that have guided this book.

Strategy provides direction. It ensures that AI is applied where it creates real value, not where it simply creates interest. Without strategy, efforts become fragmented and outcomes remain uncertain.

Ethics and security provide structure. They ensure that systems can be trusted, not only because they work, but because they work in a way that is fair, transparent, and accountable. Without this foundation, even successful systems become difficult to sustain.

Upskilling connects people to technology. It recognizes that AI does not replace human capability, but reshapes it. Organizations that invest in their people create environments where AI can be used effectively, not resisted or misunderstood.

Return on investment provides validation. It ensures that AI initiatives are not judged by what they promise, but by what they deliver. It connects effort to outcome and makes progress visible.

These pillars are not independent. They reinforce one another. Strategy without measurement lacks proof. Implementation without ethics lacks trust. Technology without people lacks adoption. Together, they form a system that supports sustainable success.

The role of leadership in this system cannot be overstated. AI does not transform organizations on its own. It amplifies the decisions, priorities, and behaviors that already exist. Leaders set the tone for how AI is understood, how it is used, and how its risks are managed. They create the clarity that aligns teams, the discipline that guides execution, and the accountability that ensures results.

This is why the journey toward becoming an intelligent organization is not primarily technical. It is organizational. It requires a shift in how decisions are made, how value is measured, and how change is managed. It requires the ability to move from ideas to outcomes, from experimentation to execution, and from isolated success to scalable capability.

There is also a practical truth that must be acknowledged. Not every AI initiative will succeed. Some will fall short, others will need to be redesigned, and a few may need to be abandoned. This is not failure. It is part of the process. What matters is whether the organization learns from these experiences and applies those lessons to future efforts. Over time, this learning becomes a competitive advantage.

The future of AI within organizations will not be defined by single breakthroughs, but by consistent application. The companies that lead will be those that build systems that work, processes that support them, and cultures that sustain them. They will be the ones that understand that AI is not a destination, but a capability that evolves over time.

As you reach the end of this book, the focus shifts from understanding to action. The principles are clear. The structure is defined. The question now is how they will be applied.

Start with one initiative. Define the problem clearly. Align it with a meaningful goal. Ensure that it is implemented responsibly. Prepare the people who will work with it.

Measure its impact in terms that matter to the business. Learn from the outcome and refine the approach.

Then repeat. This is how transformation happens. Not through isolated efforts, but through consistent, disciplined execution.

The intelligent organization is not built overnight. It is built through decisions that prioritize clarity over complexity, responsibility over speed, and value over activity. It is built by leaders who understand that technology is only one part of the equation, and that lasting success depends on how that technology is guided, integrated, and sustained.

Artificial intelligence will continue to evolve. New tools will emerge, capabilities will expand, and expectations will grow. But the foundations outlined in this book will remain relevant, because they are not tied to a specific technology. They are tied to how organizations create value.

In the end, the goal is not simply to adopt AI.

It is to use it in a way that makes the organization more effective, more resilient, and more capable of navigating change.

That is what defines an intelligent organization.

And that is what you now have the foundation to build

REFERENCES:

Core AI Strategy & Business

1. Davenport, T. H., & Ronanki, R. (2018). Artificial intelligence for the real world. *Harvard Business Review, 96*(1), 108–116.
2. Iansiti, M., & Lakhani, K. R. (2020). *Competing in the age of AI*. Harvard Business Review Press.
3. Brynjolfsson, E., & McAfee, A. (2017). *Machine, platform, crowd*. W. W. Norton.
4. Westerman, G., Bonnet, D., & McAfee, A. (2014). *Leading digital*. Harvard Business Review Press.
5. McKinsey Global Institute. (2023). *The state of AI in 2023*.
6. Bughin, J., Seong, J., Manyika, J., Chui, M., & Joshi, R. (2018). *Notes from the AI frontier*. McKinsey Global Institute.
7. Fountaine, T., McCarthy, B., & Saleh, T. (2019). Building the AI-powered organization. *Harvard Business Review*.
8. Ransbotham, S., Kiron, D., LaFountain, B., Khodabandeh, S., & Winkler, R. (2022). *Achieving scale with AI*. MIT Sloan.

9. Floridi, L., et al. (2018). AI4People—An ethical framework for a good AI society. *Minds and Machines, 28*(4), 689–707.
10. Jobin, A., Ienca, M., & Vayena, E. (2019). The global landscape of AI ethics guidelines. *Nature Machine Intelligence, 1*(9), 389–399.
11. Mittelstadt, B. D., et al. (2016). The ethics of algorithms. *Big Data & Society.*
12. European Commission. (2021). *Ethics guidelines for trustworthy AI.*
13. OECD. (2019). *OECD principles on artificial intelligence.*
14. IBM Security. (2023). *Cost of a data breach report.*
15. ENISA. (2021). *Artificial intelligence cybersecurity challenges.*
16. Goodfellow, I., McDaniel, P., & Papernot, N. (2018). Making ML robust against adversarial inputs. *Communications of the ACM.*
17. MITRE. (2023). *Adversarial threat landscape for AI systems.*
18. Voigt, P., & Von dem Bussche, A. (2017). *The EU GDPR: A practical guide*. Springer.
19. Kuner, C. (2017). *Transborder data flows and data*

20. World Economic Forum. (2020). *The future of jobs report.*
21. Bessen, J. (2019). AI and jobs*: The role of demand. NBER Working Paper.*
22. Brynjolfsson, E., Rock, D., & Syverson, C. (2021). The productivity J-curve. *American Economic Journal.*
23. privacy law. Oxford University Press.
24. Sculley, D., et al. (2015). Hidden technical debt in ML systems. *NeurIPS.*
25. Amershi, S., et al. (2019). Software engineering for ML. *IEEE Software*.
26. Russell, S., & Norvig, P. (2021). *Artificial intelligence: A modern approach* (4th ed.). Pearson.

www.ingramcontent.com/pod-product-compliance
Lightning Source LLC
LaVergne TN
LVHW080530210926
848481LV00019B/810